1000 Full Moons

The Śatābhiṣeka Celebration of Guru Muni Narayana Prasad

1000 Full Moons

The Śatābhiṣeka Celebration of Guru Muni Narayana Prasad

Edited by
Vyasa Prasad

D K PRINTWORLD
Publishers of Indian Traditions

Cataloging in Publication Data — DK
[Courtesy: D.K. Agencies (P) Ltd. <docinfo@dkagencies.com>]

1000 full moons : the śatābhiṣeka celebration of Guru
Muni Narayana Prasad / edited by Vyasa Prasad.
pages cm
"Narayana Gurukula."
ISBN 9788124611579

1. Narayana Prasad, Muni, 1938- 2. Hindu philosophy.
3. Vedanta. I. Narayana Prasad, Muni, 1938- honouree.
II. Prasad, Vyasa, editor. III. Narayana Gurukula. IV. Title:
One thousand full moons. V. Title: Thousand full moons.

LCC BL1175.N37A14 2022 | DDC 181.4 23

ISBN: 978-81-246-1157-9

First published in India in 2022

Published by:
Narayana Gurukula
Sreenivasapuram PO,
Varkala - 695145 (Kerala)

and

D.K. Printworld (P) Ltd.
Regd office: "Vedaśrī", F-395, Sudarshan Park
ESI Hospital Metro Station, New Delhi - 110015
Phones: (011) 2545 3975, 2546 6019
e-mail: indology@dkprintworld.com
Web: www.dkprintworld.com

Printed by: D.K. Printworld (P) Ltd., New Delhi

Contents

Introduction

A *GURU* is a contemplative man of Wisdom. He combines science and mysticism in the neutral value that he represents in his person. He is understandable only in the context of absolutism, his visible aspects being only incidental.

This anthology, written by students and admirers of Guru Muni Narayana Prasad, is an offering of appreciation and gratitude on the auspicious occasion of his *Śatābhiṣeka,* celebrated in India as an important event in one's life. It is indeed a glorious milestone marking a lifetime of absolute dedication to the cause of Guruhood in general and to the life and teachings of Narayana Guru in particular.

This Introduction is rather fluid and impressionistic, leaving the reader to discover details and depth in the articles themselves. The opening article "Narayana Guru: Philosopher and Yogin" by Guru Muni Narayana Prasad himself presents the integral vision of Narayana Guru in a comprehensive and succinct manner, touching on his most important contributions. Kierkegaard observes that "Truth always rests with the minority … because … the strength of a majority is illusory". C.J. Jung also writes that a group experience takes place at a lower level of consciousness than the experience of an individual. Guru Muni has taken pains to establish Narayana Guru's contemplative vision thereby correcting the distortion inevitable in public understanding. Guru Muni's penetration into Upaniṣadic paradoxes to reveal the underlying truth is well presented in "Interpretation of Īśāvāsya Mantras" by K.P. Sreedevi. B. Sugeetha's article "Ontological and Axiological Vision in Brahmavidyā Pañcakam" presents Narayana Guru's ability to apply Occam's Razor and spells out the essence of Śaṅkara's Vedānta just in five verses. Swami Tanmaya touches upon the important topic of *bhakti,* so crucial in spiritual life. His "Contemplative Devotion" elucidates Narayana Guru's contemplative vision of *bhakti.* Next, S. Omana's "Nataraja Guru" highlights his extraordinary efforts to introduce Narayana Guru's teachings in an idiom understandable to the modern world. Swami Vyasa Prasad explores "What is this?" through "In the Stream of Consciousness". The field of education offers a fertile ground for applying the teachings of the Guru. Humanity requires a healing education which returns man to himself. In her article, "Education and Self-Realization in the Light of Narayana Guru's Wisdom Teachings", Anjumol V. reunites education with Self-realization, thereby bridging the rift caused by modern dualism. Her article applies the educational theories of Nataraja Guru. Satyabai Sivadas' erudition and imagination is evident in her original writing, "A Modern Myth".

Narayana Guru's universal vision transcends notions such as East and West. Scott Teitsworth has written an original and refreshing reflection, "Gee You Are You Too". Deborah Buchanen's article, "Moments by the River", presents her interesting understanding of the three successors of Narayana Guru as "intellectual and revolutionary", "psychological and contemplative", "open and generous". This should help any seeker who feels bewildered by the Gurukula *paramparā.* Andy Larkin's article,

"Sacred Art" introduces us to the spiritual in art. In fact, Narayana Guru, in the middle of the *Adhyāropa Darśana* compares the picturesque variety of the world to the work of God as an artist, *citrakāravat bhagavān*. These articles establish Narayana Guru's global vision.

Personal encounters with Guruhood are depicted by Satyabai Sivadas' autobiographical "How My Guru Revealed Himself to Me" and Swami Vyasa Prasad's "Close Encounters with the Fourth Dimension", a narration of his encounters with the Guru in his quest for a stable and meaningful life.

Articles of appreciation include, "Narayana Guru's Prasādam" by Deepanjali and "Basic Lessons on India's Wisdom" by Pooja Lal, a third-year Biology student at Temple University, USA, a representative of the youthful world.

Narayana Guru not only revised and revalued the epistemology, methodology and axiology of Vedānta, but also liberated the denominator base of humanity and corrected diehard social prejudice. Moving, as it were, from core teachings to encounters in the the world of social action, C.M. Neelakandhan advocates empowerment of youth in his article, "Philosophical Traditions of India and the Empowerment of Youth from the Viewpoint of Swami Vivekananda". In keeping with the progressive spirit of the times, Acharyasri has presented a new possibility for spiritual renaissance, drawing from the examples of both Christ and Narayana Guru, in his article, "An Advaitic Christology and Liberative Spirituality for Integral Renaissance of India".

Finally, we arrive at poetry. The poets should probably be presented first, as poetry is the original and ancient form of self-expression. Swami Tyageswaran captures the universal essence and elevates the reader through his poems, "Caitanya Jyotis" and "Maha Guru", while Rani Jayachandran's "Rain Inside" and "A Silent Seeker" draw us into the inner chamber of appreciation.

This Introduction would be incomplete without acknowledging the aesthetic cover designed by Andy Larkin, based on verse 15 of *Ātmopadeśa Śatakam:*

To the blessed ones who have sucked the milk of parā
ten thousand years is but a moment;
but if knowledge succumbs to aparā prakṛti
half a second seems like a thousand years.

We once again profusely thank D.K. Printworld for publishing a fine edition worthy of appreciation.

We began with a quote from the writings of Nataraja Guru, and we end by closing the bracket with his fitting tribute to the notion of Guruhood:

> Our adoration to all *guru*s who've come and gone, to all who had the strange, mysterious silence of the Word on their features. The earth has been sanctified by the touch of these *guru*s. Each has tried hard to live up to the best standards of the *guru* tradition, adding their share to the accumulated wealth of Word-wisdom as a heritage for humanity. Praise be to all of them, those dauntless unperturbed spirits, representatives of the human race of whom we can never be too proud, those who were replete with wisdom's Word. They are the common fathers of humanity, with One High Absolute for ideal, one religion for commonweal to follow and one solid human fraternity to which all belong. Praise be to the *guru*s, known or unknown, who have consciously or unconsciously represented the glory of the articulated or inarticulated *AUṀ*.

Narayana Gurukula
Fernhill
4 November 2021

Swami Vyasa Prasad

Guru Muni Narayana Prasad

GURU Muni Narayana Prasad was born on 9 December 1938 at Nagaroor, near Attingal in Thiruvananthapuram district, Kerala, India as the son of a primary school teacher. His real name happens to be M.N. Prasad. He had his initial schooling at the same school where his father was the headmaster. After passing the 10th standard he pursued studies at a technical institute preparing for one-year course in civil engineering. He came in contact with Swami Nitya Chaitanya Yati and from 1955 started associating with the Narayana Gurukula movement. After a short training at Thiruvananthapuram Engineering College he entered Kerala government service as a draughtsman in 1958. He continued with his government job while staying at the Varkala Gurukula during this period.

On 21 January 1970 he was conferred *brahmacarya dīkṣā* by Nataraja Guru and joined the lineage of the Gurukula. Nataraja Guru gave him the name Muni Narayana Prasad. After resigning from his government job he began a dedicated life at the Gurukula.

When Nataraja Guru convened the World Parliament of Religions at Sasthamkotta, Kerala, in 1971, Muni Narayana Prasad was the organizing secretary. He also conducted the Conference for World Peace through

Unitive Understanding held at Ezhimala, convened by Nataraja Guru. He functioned as the editor of the Malayalam *Gurukulam* magazine from 1973 to 1989.

In 1985 he was given *saṁnyāsa dīkṣā* by Guru Nitya Chaitanya Yati. Among his overseas engagements, he has participated in the round-table meet of world religious leaders at Moscow in February 1987. He was the head of the Geeta Ashram in Fiji Islands from 1989 to end of June 1991. He has visited several countries and given classes in the US, Malaysia, Australia, England, Russia and in many Gulf countries.

After the *samādhi* of Guru Nitya on 14 May 1999, he took charge as Guru and Head of the Narayana Gurukula movement. A prolific writer, he has authored more than 100 books in English and Malayalam which include commentaries on the entire works of Narayana Guru, 10 principal Upaniṣads and the *Bhagavadgītā*. He has accomplished the difficult task of commenting on the complete works of Narayana Guru, as well as translating all of them into English. This great achievement is an invaluable contribution to humanity.

English Works

INDEPENDENT WORKS

1. *Karma and Reincarnation*, 1994
2. *Basic Lessons on India's Wisdom*
3. *Functional Democracy: A Failure in India*
4. *Children's Narayana Guru*
5. *The Philosophy of Narayana Guru*, 2003
6. *Pure Philosophy Simplified for the Youth*, 2011

7. *Christ the Guru*, 2014
8. *Three Ācāryas and Narayana Guru*, 2011
9. *Gurukula Dhyāna Mañjūṣā: A Bouquet of Meditations* (Compilation)

COMMENTARIES

1. *Life's Pilgrimage through the Gītā*, 2005
2. *Vedānta Sūtras of Narayana Guru*, 1997
3. *Vedānta upto Narayana Guru*
4. *Iśāvāsya Upaniṣad*, 2009
5. *Kena Upaniṣad*, 1995
6. *Kaṭha Upaniṣad*, 1998
7. *Praśna Upaniṣad*, 1999
8. *Muṇḍaka Upaniṣad*, 1998
9. *Māṇḍūkya Upaniṣad*, 2009
10. *Taittirīya Upaniṣad*, 1994
11. *Aitareya Upaniṣad*, 2000
12. *Chāndogya Upaniṣad*, 2006
13. *The Complete Works of Narayana Guru*
14. *Garland of Visions* (An Extensive Commentary Based on the *Darśana Mālā* of Narayana Guru), 2007
15. *Ātmopadeśa Śatakam* (Hindi), 1999
16. *Life and Lessons with a Guru* (Memories)
17. *Shoter Philosophical Poems of Narayana Guru*, 2010

The English works were published by D.K. Printworld, New Delhi.

Malayalam Works

Besides the above books in English, he has authored about 75 books in Malayalam. They include independent works, commentaries and translations from English to Malayalam. In his autobiography he says that in order to study any book in detail, he either wrote a commentary or translated it.

INDEPENDENT WORKS

1. *Nyāyadarśanam*, 1976
2. *Hindumaththile Śāstravīkṣaṇam*, 1983
3. *Pūrṇajananam* (collection of essays), 1989
4. *Mīmāṁsādarśanangal*, 2006
5. *Gurukula Dhyānamañjūṣā* (a bouquet of prayers and hymens for Gurukula disciples)
6. *Kuttikalude Narayana Guru* (*Biography of Narayana Guru for Children*), 2006
7. *Greek Chinthakar* (*Greek Philosophers*), 1987
8. *Arivinte Aadyapadaṅgaḷ*, 1990
9. *Karamavum Punarjanmavum*, 1985
10. *Vedāntam Narayana Guru Vare*, 2001
11. *Subhāṣithaṅgaḷ*, 2005
12. *Oru Guru Śiṣyabandham*, 2007
13. *Ātmayānam* (Autobiography), 2015
14. *Yuvadarśanam*, 2012
15. *Bhagavat Gītāyum Ātmopadeśathamavum*, 2008
16. *Narmaṅgaḷ Marmaṅgaḷ*, 2016

17. *Kochu Valiyakaryaṅgaḷ*, 2018
18. *Manas Vasiṣṭathil*, 2015
19. *Sree Naryana Gurudevakrithikal School Pandangaḷ*, 2014
20. *Suviśeṣaṅgal Vedānta Dṛṣṭiyil*, 2009
21. *Brahmasūtra Bhāṣyavum Jāthiyum*, 2004
22. *Narayana Guruvinte Advaithadarśanam*, 1993
23. *Arivinte Kalimuttam*, 2012
24. *Bhakthi*, 2021
25. *Gurudarśanam Oru Ethinottam*, 2019
26. *Nooru Daivanāmaṅgaḷ*, 2018
27. *Allahuvinte Nāmathil*, 2021

COMMENTARIES

1. *Complete Works of Narayana Guru*, 2019
2. *Jīvithaparyadānam Gīthāyilude*, 2007
3. *Aṣṭavakra Gītā*, 2009
4. *Dakṣiṇamūrthi Sthotram*, 2016
5. *Īśāvāśya Upaniṣad*
6. *Kena Upaniṣad*
7. *Kaṭha Upaniṣad*
8. *Praśna Upaniṣad*
9. *Muṇḍaka Upaniṣad*
10. *Māṇḍūkya Upaniṣad*
11. *Taittirīya Upaniṣad*

12. *Aitareya Upaniṣad*
13. *Chāndogya Upaniṣad*
14. *Śvethāśvathara Upaniṣad*

TRANSLATIONS

1. *Guruvaruḷ* (*Word of the Guru* – 2nd part), 2001
2. *Nataraja Guruvinte Ātmakathā* (*Autobiography of Nataraja Guru* – 3rd and 4th parts)
3. *Ātmopadeśaśathakam* (translation of Nataraja Guru's commentary – from verse 27 onwards), 1983
4. *Satyānveṣanam* (Henri Bergson's *An Introduction to Metaphysics*), 2002
5. *Kadalrañchi* (Richard Bach's *Jonathan Livingston*)
6. *Kunjunnirājaṇ* (Antoine de Saint Exupery's *The Little Prince*), 1984
7. *Saundarya Laharī* (translation of Nataraja Guru's commentary), 2003
8. *Oru Guruvinte Satyadarśanam* (translation of Nataraja Guru's *The Philosophy of a Guru*), 1990
9. *Vedāntam: Oru Punareekshanam* (translation of Nataraja Guru's *Vedānta Revalued and Restated*), 2007
10. *Paramporul Pāścāthya Darśanathil* (translation of Nataraja Guru's *Search for a Norm in Western Thought*), 2008
11. *Brahmavidyā Sarvavidyā Prathiṣṭha* (translation of Nataraja Guru's *Integrated Science of the Absolute*), 2003
12. *Vedānta Paribhāṣā* (Dharmarāja Adharyu's work), 2010
13. *Ekaloka Sampathikaśāstram* (translation of Nataraja Guru's *Towards a One world Economics*), 2013

1

Narayana Guru
Philosopher and Yogin

Muni Narayana Prasad

Section I: A Philosopher

THE word "philosophy" means "to love wisdom" (Greek *philein*, to love + *sophia*, wisdom). Philosophy includes every area of human interest within its purview and, hence, it is "the most general science". The *Random House Dictionary* defines philosophy as "The rational investigation of the truth and principles of being, knowledge and conduct". In other words, philosophy deals with Ultimate Reality, the nature of knowledge and a person's conduct in conformity with this understanding. Both "the means of attaining wisdom" and "the content of wisdom" are included within philosophy, whether Eastern or Western.

Rational thinking, the accepted method of scientific investigation, is also the means adopted for the study of philosophy. Rational thinking is formulated by the human mind, but is the human mind formulated with the help of rational thinking? Is the human mind capable of rationally knowing the reality that conceived and assumed the form of the mind and its rational thinking? The answer to these questions is "no".

Narayana Guru ponders on that Ultimate Reality thus:

Boundless, indeterminate and beyond the grasp of mind and words,
How could the course of right reason move within its domain?

– *Ātmopadeśa Śatakam*, verse 94

Sat

The Ultimate Being is known as *sat* in Indian philosophy. *Sat* transcends the distinction between individual beings (*jīvas*), the universal reality (*jagat*) and God (*Īśvara*). Pondering on this non-dual Being, the Guru says:

jīveśvara-jagad-bheda-rahita advaita tejase

(Salutations) to the non-dual effulgence that is beyond the distinction of individual souls, God and the world.

– *Daiva Cintanam* part II

Cit

After *sat* let us examine the domain of knowledge. Knowledge as understood in Western philosophy is one of the functional facets within the all-inclusive *cit* (unconditioned Consciousness), in Vedānta. *Cit* attains its absolute dimension in the intuitive experience of the knower, the known and knowledge being absorbed into their intrinsic oneness. Narayana Guru says:

Knowledge, the object known and the person's knowledge together make one primeval effulgence.

– *Ātmopadeśa Śatakam*, verse 4

Ānanda

The third element understood within the scope of Western philosophy is proper conduct to ensure happiness in life. This is considered to be one aspect of the all-inclusive value-sense called *ānanda* in Vedānta. The *ānanda* experience ranges from ordinary sense pleasures at the lower limit to the non-dual bliss at the highest where the enjoyer and the enjoyed become interchangeable. Realizing the upper limit of *ānanda* as one's own self-content gives the experience of immortality – the one birthless and deathless Reality. Thus, the ultimate goal one can attain is realizing oneself as *sat–cit–ānanda* or *saccidānanda*. Narayana Guru confirms this vision in the following words:

> *Neither that, nor this, nor the content of existence am I;*
> *But Existence, Consciousness, Joy Immortal – thus attaining clarity,*
> *Emboldened, discarding attachments to being and non-being,*
> *One should gently gently merge in SAT AUṀ.*
>
> – *Ātmopadeśa Śatakam*, verse 100

In view of the above, philosophy in India is not merely "Love of Wisdom", but a *darśana* (vision).

How Is This Wisdom to Be Attained?

The essential Reality in the being of oneself is none other than that Reality. This inconceivable Reality self-unfolds as various triads such as "being–knowledge–conduct", "individual being–universal being–God", "knower–known–knowledge", "here–hereafter–the midworld", *sattva–rajas–tamas*" (three *guṇa*s or nature modalities that constitute *prakṛti* or nature) and "gross–subtle–causal". Therefore, the most direct and easiest way to know or attain that Reality is by knowing oneself in terms of one's essential content. In other words, Self-knowledge is the best way to attain the final goal.

Narayana Guru's *Ātmopadeśa Śatakam* (*One Hundred Verses of Self-*

Instruction) is a search for the Self (*ātmā*). The word *ātmā* means "oneself" as well as "the all-pervading substance". Everything perceivable and conceivable is visualized as non-different from the One Self, or as various functional facets of one and the same Consciousness-Reality. The word *Brahman* does not appear in the work though it presents *brahma-vidyā* (Science of Absolute).

The Guru's epoch-making Sanskrit work *Vedānta Sūtras* is also a search for *ātmā* (*ātmā-jijñāsā*) rather than a desire to know *Brahman* (Absolute) (*brahma-jijñāsā*). This is the first *sūtra* text on Vedānta written since Bādarāyaṇa's *Vedāntasūtras* or *Brahmasūtras* of ancient times. Narayana Guru is a continuator of the same tradition as is evident from his own words: "As Upaniṣadic secret lore declares" (*Ātmopadeśa Śatakam*, verse 14).

All the Upaniṣads follow the same method of enquiry, investigating one or other aspect of *ātmā*. The *Śvetāśvatara Upaniṣad* II.15 acknowledges this method as proper to Vedānta:

yad ātmatattvena tu brahmatattvaṁ

For the *Brahman*-Reality is to be attained by knowing the *ātmā*-Reality.

A Unique Way of Self-Enquiry

Unlike ancient *ṛṣis* and later commentators like Śaṅkara, Narayana Guru fully conforms with the spirit of the Age of Science in which he lived and taught. To inquire into the Self and its nature he adopts a method of a controlled "laboratory experiment". The "laboratory" is a dark room in which two people are sitting, unable to see each other. Suspecting the presence of someone else in the room, one asks, "Who is sitting in darkness?" In reply the other person in turn asks, "Who may even you be?" The reply to both questioners is one alone, viz. "I", the common content of the first person singular.

What is the common "I" in both? This "I" should be common to everyone else as well. At the same time, each also has a separate "I"-sense comprising all the fleeting elements that form the physical body as well as the subtler inner faculties, along with their functions.

These two kinds of "I"-sense find their unity in the neutral being of each of us. This neutral "I" is related to the individual being on one side and to the cosmic being on the other. The non-dual Self in which both these conceivable self-aspects find their unity is what we are seeking.

What is the essential content of that non-dual Self-being? Experientially, it is the "I"-sense which has the feeling of possession, or "mine": my body, my senses, my mind and even my self, and in relation with external existence, my world, my country, my family, my things. This is very familiar to us, but who is the possessor that feels all these as "mine"? It is merely an awareness or consciousness of one's own beingness, which has no existence other than pure and unconditioned Consciousness called *cit* in Sanskrit. The word the Guru uses to signify this Reality is *arivu.* As my own existence is an integral part of cosmic being, what is real in "me" has to be the real substance in the cosmic being also. That means, *cit* or *arivu* is itself the one Reality that underlies the being of an individual as well as of the universe.

Is Ultimate Reality the substance in the being of the individual entity or the substance in the universal entity? Neither, they are like the two sides of one coin. The non-dual Reality has to be visualized where these two facets of existence find their inseparable unity.

It is here that the great dicta (*mahāvākya*s) of Vedānta become meaningful and come to our aid. The primary one being *tat-tvam-asi* (That-Thou-Art), in which the individual being is signified by the word *tvam* (Thou) and the universal being by *tat* (That).

This *mahāvākya* is given like an equation (*tat* = *tvam*). While every equation has two limbs, the meaning that is grasped is not the meaning of either of the limbs, but the inexpressible oneness of the two limbs (which is not actually written). Thus, what is stated are the two limbs of the equation and what is grasped is something other than the two, and is not stated. The same is true with the equation *tat* = *tvam* or *tat-tvam-asi* also. It is not the meaning denoted by *tat* nor by *tvam* that is meant to be meditatively visualized, but their unstated oneness is to be intuitively perceived.

Narayana Guru directly makes reference to the other *mahāvākya*s also (*aham brahmāsmi, ayam ātmā brahma* and *prajñānam brahma*), in the form of equations in his Sanskrit work *Brahmavidyā Pañcakam* (*The Science of the Absolute in Five Verses*). The teachings of a *ṛsi* like Narayana Guru being extremely subtle and hidden, it is no wonder that his words are not correctly appraised by many. The Guru makes reference to the extremely elusive nature of the Wisdom he represents with these words:

> *Such the supreme secret of the* paṇḍita *(wise man), who is here to see it?*
> – *Ātmopadeśa Śatakam*, verse 63

A Logical Approach

The Guru, in yet another context, adopts the method of pure logical thinking to arrive at the conclusion that Pure Consciousness alone has real existence.

When we examine our direct perception or conception of the world, we find that what we perceive or conceive are the distinguishing features and attributes, but not the possessor of these attributes. The substance that possesses these attributes is never perceived or conceived. Yet, the existence of a substance is undeniable, for without a substance, no attribute can appear to be.

What is this substance and how does it exist? That unseen substance which can neither be perceived nor conceived, but has undeniable existence, has to be in our awareness. That which exists in awareness alone and nowhere else has to be Consciousness in essence. This substance is called *dharmin* by the Guru and its attributes are called *dharma.* To quote his own words:

Whatever is known is not the dharmin,
But only are dharmas, *for the said* dharmin
Remains imperceptible;
The earth and the like, therefore,
Do not have real being;
What really exists is
The One all-supporting arivu,
Do recall constantly.
– *Ātmopadeśa Śatakam*, verse 32

An Analytical Method

In keeping with the spirit of the modern age, the Guru adopts an analytical method to demonstrate that Consciousness alone is the all-underlying substance. His own words in verse 3 of the *Advaita Dīpikā* (*Lamp of Non-duality*) are self-explanatory:

Cloth is nothing but yarn,
Yarn is nothing but cotton fibres,
And fibres turn to be but primeval
Elements clinging together;

This way of search extended to its extreme,
Reveals that everything becomes apparent
Out of one Consciousness,
Comparable to the flow of mirage-waters seen in desert lands;
Ultimately Consciousness alone does exist.

The same idea is reiterated in verse 7 of the Apavāda-Darśana in the Sanskrit work *Darśanamālā* by the Guru:

> *When everything is divided on and on into parts, then what is perceived at the end of that is: all is but Pure Consciousness (cit) alone, far from the delusions of māyā and nothing else is seen.*

From the Common-sense Point of View

According to our common-sense point of view, the world outside exists different from us. Such a notion is derived from our sense perception, which is but one of our experiences. But when closely examined, every experience is felt within our consciousness and one cannot think of the existence of a world outside one's experience. Thus, the materiality and externality of objects are in our experience. Therefore, all experiences are simply different functional modes of Consciousness. Pointing to this aspect, the Guru in the Yoga-Darśana of *Darśanamālā* says:

> *dṛśyasya na dṛśo 'stitvam ato dṛśyam dṛgātmakam*
>
> – verse IX.7

> Perceived objects have no existence of their own, therefore, the perceived objects are perceiving consciousness in essence.

This Consciousness-Reality is basically one alone as we have already seen.

Ātmā

The word *ātmā* literally means "that which pervades the being of everything (*āpnoti iti ātmā*)". *Ātmā* also means The substance assuming the form of oneself. This *ātmā,* in line with the Upaniṣadic teachings, is Pure Consciousness (*cit*) in essential content.

Vedāntic textbooks, including the Upaniṣads, do not give a positive definition of *ātmā,* but define it negatively in terms of what it is not. Narayana Guru in his *Ātmopadeśa Śatakam* (verse 27) defines *ātmā* positively in experiential terms. The verse, along with the definition, states how *ātmā* mysteriously appears as everything that constitutes the world. The verse reads:

> *That which is conscious of itself*
> *Even when in darkness is the* ātmā*,*
> *Itself is* arivu*, and it manifests*
> *As all the names and forms,*
> *As all mental faculties and senses,*
> *As all* karmas *and their doers,*
> *Lo and behold*! *what a great magic all this is*!

The World Appearance

Ātmā (One Consciousness-Reality), owing to its own immense creative potential called *māyā,* unfolds itself and assumes the form of the world having both subjective (*ahantā*) and objective (*idantā*) aspects. All the involuntary and voluntary actions (*karmas*) take place as an expression of this creative urge inherent in the one *ātmā*. The Guru in his *Darśanamālā* (VI.1) categorically says:

ātmaiva māyayā karma karoti bahurūpa-dhṛk ।
asaṅgaḥ svaprakāśo 'pi nidrāyām iva taijasaḥ ॥

Ātmā alone, while being self-luminous and unattached to anything, performs all *karmas* by assuming numerous forms owing to its own *māyā*.

Thus, people think that they have their own *karmas* due to ignorance about what and who they really are. Thinking that one has one's own *karmas* pertain to the realm of world appearance.

The world appearance has no existence of its own apart from the all-inclusive existence of *ātmā*, just as waves and ocean have no being other than the water-content in both. Waves are individuated apparent forms, while the ocean is the universal aspect of the same water. Just as the actuality of the waves is not denied, the actuality of the world appearance is also not denied.

Certain activities that take place within *ātmā* itself appear as the ever-changing world. This active state of the existence of *ātmā* is called *prakṛti*, loosely translatable as "nature". *Prakṛti*, a term vital to the Sāṁkhya system, lacked a proper definition. Narayana Guru provided a definition of *prakṛti* as follows:

karotīti prakarṣeṇa prakṛtyaiva guṇān pṛthak ।
nigadyate 'sau prakṛtir-itīha triguṇātmika ॥
– *Darśanamālā* IV.10

In the sense that it, by its own nature, separates out *guṇas* in its own proper way, it is well known as *prakṛti*, having three *guṇas* in essential content.

The *kṛti* (activity) of *prakṛti* results in the separation of several dual aspects, such as *ahantā* and *idantā* (subjective and objective aspects of the apparent world), the enjoyer (*bhoktā*) and the enjoyed (*bhogya*), the doer (*kartā*) and the action (*karma*). The mysterious potential in the one *ātmā* or Consciousness-Reality to become self-unfolded as the world appearance is known as *māyā* in Vedānta. *Māyā* results in phenomenal dualities which hide Reality from our view, rendering us ignorant of its unity. *Māyā* thus has the ontological function of causing the appearance of the world and the epistemological function of rendering us ignorant about the Real.

The "Why" of the World

We have seen how the world originates from the one *ātmā*. But why does it happen? Why can't *ātmā* remain as such without unfolding? This basic question has not been asked in the normal course of Vedānta. Narayana Guru gives an answer in verse 33 of the *Ātmopadeśa Śatakam:*

> Arivu, *in order to ferret out its own proper nature,*
> *Itself the earth and other manifestations becomes,*
> *Thus in upturning state, now mounting, now changing over,*
> *Like a circulating fire-faggot, it keeps turning round.*

As was seen earlier, *ātmā* is *sat* in essence, *cit* in essence and also *ānanda* in essence. These three latent aspects express themselves so that *ātmā* could have the enjoyment of self-expression. This is an actualization of *ātmā*'s own *ānanda* content and is accomplished by unfolding itself in numerous ways, unique to itself, resulting in the world appearance. It is comparable to a small child at play, making many things out of whatever comes to hand and then destroying them. The child enjoys expressing and seeing all the potentials that hide within itself. So too is the case with *ātmā*. In fact, every activity we naturally engage in is aimed at experiencing the happiness of self-expression. No one, including the *ātmā*-Reality, can stop the inner urge from directly seeing the possibilities that hide within oneself.

No Escapism

Vedānta is often misrepresented as a philosophy of escapism. But neither the Upaniṣadic *ṛsis* nor Narayana Guru consider the actualities of life as unreal. Rather, all actualities are seen as having existence inseparable from the all-inclusive Existence, *cit* or *arivu.* The *Chāndogya Upaniṣad* says *ātmaivedam sarvam* (everything here indeed is *ātmā*). The actuality of waves is not denied, but is affirmed as one with the being of ocean.

Vedānta does not expect running away from the actualities of life and its problems. All the perils and pleasures are meant to be faced with a peaceful and bold state of mind resulting from the basic understanding that all such experiences are possible in the unpredictable and mysterious way in which the *ātmā*-Reality creatively exists. Perceiving a particular facet of the one Reality in every situation in life, whether serious or insignificant, provides us with a new attitude towards life. It is not the actual world and its details that disappear, but our wrong understanding disappears. The Guru says:

Everything is real indeed,
but a true philosopher grasps all these as One;
When not perceived through the inward eye,
That great tribulation which is māyā
Yields much puzzlement indeed.

– *Ātmopadeśa Śatakam*, verse 88

The Guru did not run away from personal or social problems of life around him. Instead, he faced them with the attitude normal to an enlightened seer. He perceived himself as well as everything else as *arivu* in essence. He saw himself in everything and everything in himself, as taught in *Īśa Upaniṣad* verse 6. No one was "other" to him. This vision gave him the clarity and boldness to pinpoint the core of the wrongs prevailing in the society due to people's ignorance and to encourage them to correct themselves. Nevertheless, he remained unattached in the midst of all activity. Even though he sometimes appeared in gatherings, he was not mentally attached to any social issue. He even took the initiative to establish temples, schools and the like. This peculiarity of his life became the cause for historians to evaluate him as a social reformer or as the leader of Kerala's renaissance. Such people, in fact, have no intuitive perception to understand an enlightened seer's mind. Instead, they correlate externally visible events in society and the formulate historical theories based on them.

The definition of a *brahmavit* (knower of *Brahman*) found in verse 5 of the "Nirvāṇa-Darśana" of *Darśanamālā* depicts a clear picture of the Guru's life pattern, especially in the later years of his life. It reads:

> *dagdhvā jñānāgninā sarvam uddiśya jagatām hitam* ।
> *karoti vidhivat karma brahmavid brahmaṇi sthitaḥ* ।।

> Having burnt down everything in the fire of Wisdom, the *brahmavit* performs actions in conformity with prescribed rules, aiming at the good of the world, himself remaining in *Brahman*.

Such an inner state of a seer is never graspable by any historian, social leader or politician.

Knowledge

Every knowing function involves a subject and an object (*jñātā* and *jñeya*). These two, as we have just seen, are functional facets of one and the same *ātmā* becoming self-unfolded as *prakṛti* due to *māyā.* A knowing function, therefore, is really an occasion in which the subject and the object come together and realize their intrinsic oneness.

The knowing function of *ātmā* (Consciousness-Reality) is analysed by Guru in verses 36-42 of *Ātmopadeśa Śatakam.* The infinite knowing potentials latent in Consciousness are first categorized into two sets, viz. *sama* (same) and *anya* (other). The latter is the kind of knowledge that perceives many apparent forms and the former sees one Reality alone in everything. Each of these two categories has its own generic and specific aspects as well. For example, the knowledge "This is a pot" is of the *anya* kind. The "this" part is generic, because anything can be referred to as "this". But the mention of 'this' alone does not give any clarity to the concerned knowledge. Clarity is provided by predicating "is a pot". "Pot", then, is the specific aspect (*viśeṣa*) of the knowledge "This is a pot".

Closely looked at, every item of knowledge can be seen as involving a generic (*sāmānya*) and a specific (*viśeṣa*) aspect. In short, all specific objective knowledge is the outcome of an extremely subtle whirl-like interplay (*brahmakala*) that involves the togetherness of the generic and specific facets of the *anya* kind of the knowing function within the Consciousness-Reality.

The *sama* kind of knowledge perceives one Consciousness (*arivu*) alone as real in everything. It also has its own generic and specific facets. In fact, this kind of knowledge has one example alone, i.e. "This is

Consciousness". In this case also, the "this" part is generic in nature and is given specificity by the "Consciousness" part which is the *viśeṣa* aspect of the *sama* kind of knowledge. The Guru here directs us to meditate on the generic "this" aspect of the knowledge "This is Consciousness" in order to lead us to the ultimate goal (*sad-gati*) we are seeking.

Thus, the analysis of the knowing function of Consciousness guides the seeker to meditate on the Ultimate Reality (*sat*) which is the goal he or she is in search of.

Such an analysis of the knowing function of human consciousness, and making it a means to attain the final goal of life, is one of the original contributions of Narayana Guru to philosophy in general and Vedānta in particular. No *upaniṣad* or *bhāṣya* (commentaries of masters) goes into such a valuable study.

A Norm for Ethics

Ethics, a branch of philosophy, has hitherto lacked a universal and absolute norm to decide what is ethically right or wrong. This topic becomes relevant when man, one of the manifest forms of one *ātmā*, relates himself with others. As a social animal, man cannot do away with relating himself with others. The Guru deals with this delicate subject in verses 21-25 of *Ātmopadeśa Śatakam.*

All men, all beings, and everything that forms the apparent world are, as we have already seen, various forms in which the one and only *ātmā*-Reality becomes self-unfolded. Thus, all such are basically of one substance. Narayana Guru points out that this oneness of everyone serves as a standard to evaluate the ethical soundness or otherwise of human behaviour. One in substance, all hold the high value of happiness as the dearest. Therefore, what one does for self-happiness must ensure the self-happiness of others as well. To put it in Guru's own words:

The other man's interest, that is even mine; what to oneself
Is beneficial is so for the other man also: such is the course of
Discrete conduct; all acts aiming at each man's self-happiness
Must spell at once the happiness of the other fellow-man.

– Verse 22

What here we view as this man or that,
Reflection reveals to be the Self's prime form;
That conduct adopted for one's self-happiness
Another's happiness must also secure at once.

– Verse 24

This could well be considered as another of Narayana Guru's contribution to philosophy in general.

Oneness of Religions

Religions serve to guide human life when man relates himself with *prakṛti* (Nature) or with the Ultimate Reality that functions in an unpredictable and uncertain way. The Guru says:

By Nature's action caught and turned,
Men of good actions too, alas! keep turning round.

– *Ātmopadeśa Śatakam*, verse 43

Religions call the Ultimate Reality, God. Man cannot live without relating himself to this Ultimate Reality because he is an integral part of it. It is not possible to make the will of *prakṛti* or God conform with human desires in order to ensure man's happiness. The only alternative for man is to regulate his own aspirations in life in such a way that they agree with the unpredictability of *prakṛti.* Every religion teaches man in one way or another to achieve this goal. Such an effort to achieve self-happiness is made by every human being, at all times either knowingly or unknowingly. In respect of this fundamental aspect, all religions are one in essential content. In Guru's own words:

> *Every man at every time makes effort in every way*
> *Aiming at self-happiness, therefore in this world*
> *Know faith as one, understanding thus,*
> *Shunning evil, the inner self into calmness merge.*
>
> – *Ātmopadeśa Śatakam*, verse 49

Reflections on this area of human interest normally does not find place in philosophy. Narayana Guru is an exception in this respect, as evidenced in verses 43-49 of the *Ātmopadeśa Śatakam.*

Value Vision

All philosophical speculations, particularly in India, are aimed at attaining the ultimate goal of life named differently by each school. Vedānta calls it *mukti* or *mokṣa* (ultimate freedom). Narayana Guru does not use either of these words in any of his philosophical works though his goal is the same. The first and last verses of his Universal Prayer, *Daiva Daśakam* (*Ten Verses on God*), show the two facets of this ultimate goal. The first verse portrays the negative side crossing the ocean of becoming (*bhavābdhi*) or the ocean of changes (*saṁsāra*) and becoming free of the sufferings pertaining to it. The last verse, on the other hand, depicts the positive side of attaining the goal in terms of enjoying the eternal happiness of the seeker merging in the deep ocean of the Beauteous Effulgence of God or the Self and remaining everlastingly one with It. The same Goal, in philosophical terms, is depicted by Guru in verse 4 of *Ātmopadeśa Śatakam:*

> Within the cleftless radiance of that Great Consciousness One should merge and become That alone.

The same goal, in a more serene yet experiential mood, is given as the concluding verse of the same work:

> *Neither that nor this nor the content of existence am I;*
> *But Existence, Consciousness, Joy Immortal – thus attaining clarity,*
> *Emboldened, discarding attachments to being and non-being,*
> *One should gently gently merge in SAT AUṀ.*
>
> – Verse 100

Such a value experience is meant to be felt by each person individually. This Wisdom has value in the social life of man as well. We shall deal with this in "Yoga and Social Reforms".

Section II: A Yogin

Both a person in the state of *yoga* and one who practises the disciplines for attaining that *yoga* state are called *yogins*. The Guru was a *yogin* in the former sense.

The word *yoga* is derived from the root *yuj* having varied senses, such as *yuja-saṁyamane, yujir yoge,* both meaning "to make united". The same root, in the context of practised disciplines, means "to make the mind concentrated (*yuja-samādhau*)". The primary meaning of the word *yoga* according to the *Vācaspatyam,* the most authoritative Sanskrit lexicon, is *yojane* (bringing together to oneness) or *melane* (meeting together).

The union in the context of spiritual practice is between the being of the individual and the universal being, both Consciousness in essence. Separateness of the two is imagined by the human mind while trying to understand Reality.

Many are the systems prevailing and practised under the common title *yoga*. The originator of the Yoga system of philosophy is Patañjali who defined *yoga* as: *yogaḥ cittavṛtti nirodhaḥ* (*yoga* is restraining all functions of mind). *Jñāna-yoga, karma-yoga, bhakti-yoga, rāja-yoga, haṭha-yoga, laya-yoga, nāda-yoga, sahaja-yoga, kriyā-yoga* and *sudarśana-yoga* are some of the spiritual practices that come under the common umbrella of the word *yoga*. Many such practices may arise in future as well.

Narayana Guru, an enlightened seer, gives his own definition of *yoga,* treated as a spiritual practice, in the "Yoga Darśana" (chapter IX) of *Darśanamālā* (*Garland of Visions*):

> *satatam yojayati yad yunakti ca cidātmani* ।
> *mano nirodha rūpo'yam sa yoga iti śamsitaḥ* ।। – IX.1
>
> The state of mind-restraint by which one unites oneself with and becomes one with *ātmā,* Consciousness (*cit*) in essence, is praised as *yoga.*
>
> *na draṣṭā darśam dṛśyam vidyate yatra tatra hṛt* ।
> *yojayed vāsanā yāvad yogo 'yam iti yogavit* ।। – IX.2
>
> Wherein is present no distinction of perceiver, perceived and perception, therein the mind should be united as long as innate traits (*vāsanās*) prevail – this is considered as *yoga* by *yoga*-knowers.

Yoga as an enlightened awareness is defined as follows:

> *nāma-rūpam idam sarvam brahmaiveti vilīyate* ।
> *yad brahmaṇi mano nityam sa yoga iti niścitaḥ* ।। – IX.3
>
> That which is comprised of mind remaining constantly merged in

Brahman, by the realization of everything here consisting of names and forms as *Brahman* alone, is ascertained as *yoga.*

Another definition of *yoga* in more experiential terms is as follows:

cittasya taila-dhārāvad vṛttyā 'vicchinnayā 'tmani ।
nirantaram ramyate yat sa yogo yogibhiḥ smṛtaḥ ।। – IX.4

The state of incessant rejoicing in *ātmā* with a mental function unbroken like a streak of oil – this is thought of as *yoga* by *yoga*-knowers.

The Guru, as these definitions clearly show, conceived *yoga* from the perception of a Wisdom-Master. Stated otherwise, he was revisualizing the notion of *yoga* fully in line with non-dual Wisdom.

How the subjective and objective aspects of Reality find their oneness in the one *karu* (Core-Reality), which is nothing other than *ātmā,* is very clearly depicted in the first verse of *Ātmopadeśa Śatakam,* which reads as follows:

Rising even above knowledge, what radiant shines
Within the form of the knower, as equally without,
To that Core, with the eyes five restrained within,
Again and again prostrating, in adoration one should chant.

It is an instance of how the principle of *yoga* becomes a method to arrive at non-dual awareness.

Guru was well aware of the numerous prevailing sects of Yoga. A general evaluation is made by him by bringing all of them within two general categories in the concluding verse of the "Yoga-Darśana":

jñānam karmeti loke 'smin dvidhā yogaḥ samāsataḥ ।
anayor yoga vistāraḥ sarvaḥ parisamāpyate ।। IX.10

> *Yoga* in this world can be summarized as of two kinds: *jñāna-yoga* and *karma-yoga.* The entire range of Yoga is conclusively comprised within the fold of these two.

In spite of all these direct statements made by Guru in his works, many people, even biographers, evaluate him as a *yogī* who had *siddhi*s (unworldly attainments) acquired through practising *haṭha-yoga.* It is true that he had practised *haṭha-yoga* for some time as impelled by Chattampi Swami, his companion and elder brother in the spiritual pursuit, particularly in his earlier days. Later, when someone enquired about the value of *haṭha-yoga,* Guru's reaction was, "It is good enough to make phlegm come out easily".

The *haṭha-yoga* practice involves many *mudrā*s (gestures). One of them is the *khecarī-mudrā.* Guru mentions this in verse 9 of the "Yoga-Darśana" with the remark that it helps one to get rid of drowsiness, fatigue and the like.

Siddhis

Many superhuman powers seen in the life of the Guru are narrated by numerous eye witnesses as well as biographers. Most people think he attained these powers as an outcome of *yoga* practices, perhaps because Patañjali mentions such possibilities in chapter III "Vibhūti Pāda" of the *Yogasūtra.* The same *sūtra*-text also forewarns that all such *siddhi*s really are impediments to the final *siddhi, kaivalya* (aloneness or All-oneness).

All his writings testify that Narayana Guru was a *jñāna-yogī.* How then *are* the *siddhi*s seen in his actual life to be understood? He makes the point clear in verse 15 of his *Advaita Dīpikā* (*Lamp of Non-duality*) as follows:

> Ātmā *is devoid of I-sense. It, as with a* yogī,

Owing to its own māyā
Playfully unfolds itself
In various forms.
A yogī, *unmoved from his state*
Of being well-founded in yoga,
Playfully moves around
Assuming myriads of bodily forms.

The one *ātmā*-Reality has no I-sense or the sense of being the doer of anything that happens within itself. The *yogī* too, living as one with the being of the *ātmā*-Reality, has no I-sense. Because of his self-identity with the all-powerful *ātmā*, all that is possible with *ātmā* can appear in his personal being as well. Such phenomena are seen by non-*yogī*s as the *yogī*'s superhuman powers, but in the *yogī*'s own perception, he simply lives the life natural to him which others perceive as unworldly.

Yoga and Social Reforms

A real *yogin* always perceives everything that forms part of the world existing in a state of *yoga* or inseparable oneness with the one *ātmā*-Reality and thus with himself as well. This perception makes him see everything related to human life, whether individual or social, as not different from himself. Narayana Guru lived as an ideal *yogin* in this respect. When he noticed something in human life that did not agree with the oneness of Reality, he pointed it out to the people and urged them to correct themselves and teach the same to the public. His words, arising as they did from Wisdom, had an unquestionable commanding power and authoritativeness of their own, and so people always obeyed him. The activities of leaders, with Guru's support, resulted in many changes in the social life and attitude of the public in Kerala state, particularly in respect to caste-based discriminations and meaningless and unhealthy religious observances and social customs. He did not hesitate to appear personally at scenes where certain meaningless practices were actually happening so as to encourage people to correct themselves. As the low-caste people had no access to the existing traditional temples, he opened many temples by himself installing the temple deities and declaring these temples as open to all. He did all this not by coming down from the high peak of Wisdom to the level of interest in social matters. On the other hand, by remaining mentally at the peak-top, he looked at the social affairs happening down below and pointed out to the leaders the maladies that were deep rooted therein and encouraged them to uproot them.

This, in fact, is yet another facet of his Yogic *siddhi*s. A perfect *yogin,* he perceived everything of human interest as of his own interest. This can also be treated as his own way of applying his ethical vision we noticed earlier. His inner clarity as a *jñāna-yogin* found expression through remaining active in matters of general human interest. Put more simply, theory and practice together constitute the *yoga* state in a real *yogin* and Narayana Guru was a perfect example of this. Those in such a *yoga* state are named *satya-dharmās* by the *Īśa Upaniṣad.* A *jñāna-yogin* cannot live an actual life apart from a *karma-yogin* who perceives all actions as taking place in the *ātmā*-Reality and not a doer by himself. This point is clarified by Guru in the first verse of the "Karma-Darśana" (chapter VI) of *Darśanamālā* as follows:

> *ātmaiva māyayā karma karoti bahurūpa dhṛk*
>
> *Ātmā* alone, owing to *māyā,* does all actions by assuming numerous forms.

Historians, politicians and social leaders need not be expected to understand such an inner clarity of an enlightened *yogī.* Even some of the close followers of Guru did not understand him as he should be understood. So they evaluated him from the perspective familiar to them and thus began to treat him as a social reformer, as the leader of Kerala's renaissance, as the Guru of a particular community, as a *saṁnyāsī* having identity with Hinduism and so on. The wisdom he represented and lived was not meant and valuable for the people of Kerala alone; rather it is of universal and eternal value. How he perceived himself can be seen clearly in the picture of the *brahmavit* (knower of *Brahman*) he portrays in verse 5 of "Nirvāṇa-Darśana" of *Darśanamālā* which we quote here once more:

> *dagdhvā jñānāgninā sarvam uddiśya jagatām hitam*
> *karoti vidhivat karma brahmavid brahmaṇi sthitaḥ*
>
> Having burn down everything in the fire of wisdom the *brahmavit* (knower of *Brahman*) performs actions in conformity with prescribed rules of conduct aiming at the good of the world, while remaining in *Brahman.*

As is clear from this verse, a *Brahman*-knower, even when remaining active for the good of the world, retains his identity with *Brahman* and not with the society. Put otherwise, Narayana Guru's involvement in social matters is not a sign of his social commitments, rather it indicates a *yogin* in whom the *yoga* of what he knows and what he does becomes real.

Historians, social leaders and politicians, evaluating Guru as a social reformer, a particular community's *guru* or the leader of Kerala's renaissance, only expose their limitations in understanding the inner state of an enlightened *yogin.* Their interest is not in higher Wisdom which is quite unfamiliar to them. For this reason, in spite of good intention, they unwittingly pull down a *yogin* like Narayana Guru from the higher realm of identity with *Brahman* in which he remains, and perceive him as if forming part of the society and involved in the matters they are interested in. This in no way affects the pristine purity of the Wisdom of a *jñāna-yogī*. For this reason Narayana Guru, towards the end of his life, made the remark in a sad mood to his disciple Natarajan (Nataraja Guru): "You see, we do have none". The Guru intended to raise the level of the understanding of people towards the higher level of Wisdom as testified by his sublime philosophical poems, but his followers, sadly enough, pulled him down and placed him at their level of understanding and interests, and then glorified him from that standpoint.

Conclusion

Narayana Guru thus was an enlightened seer, forming a link in the long line of Upaniṣadic *ṛṣi*s. As a continuator of the perception *sarvam khalvidam brahma* (everything here indeed is *Brahman*), he gave a new dimension to Upaniṣadic wisdom fully in line with the Age of Science in which he lived. He lived as a perfect *yogin* in whom *jñāna* (wisdom) and *karma* (action) became dialectical counterparts of the philosophy he lived. As aptly put by the well-known writer Romain Rolland, "He was a *jñānī* of action".

തീർത്ഥാടകർക്ക് സ്വാഗതം
എല്ലാവർക്കും എപ്പോഴും
ശബരി ചായ
സന്ദർശിക്കുക ശബരി റ്റീ സ്റ്റാൾ

2

The Interpretation of Īśāvāsya Mantras

Observations of Muni Narayana Prasad

K.P. Sreedevi

Among the ten principle Upaniṣads, *Īśāvāsya* stands unique because it is the only one that has come down to us as part of the Saṁhitā. It forms the last chapter, i.e. the 40th chapter, of the *Śuklayajurveda Saṁhitā*. It is, therefore, also known as the *Mantropaniṣad* or *Saṁhitopaniṣad*. All the thirty-nine chapters of this Saṁhitā deal with the description of the performance of different types of *yajña*s and so this part is fully related to *karma-kāṇḍa*. But Śaṅkara says that the last chapter which starts with the *mantra īśāvāsyamidaṁ sarvaṁ* deals with the discussion of *ātma-vidyā* and so this part is called Upaniṣad:

> *īśāvāsyaṁ ityādayo hi mantrāḥ karmasu aviniyuktāḥ* ।
> *teṣāṁ akarmaśeṣasyātmano yāthātmyaprakāśanāt* ।

Though this Upaniṣad is very short in form, containing only eighteen *mantras*, it has in-depth dimensions in its content. As it aims at propagating the need of the synthesis between *jñāna* and *karma* (wisdom and action), in worldly life, it can be considered as the most important Upaniṣad as far as practical philosophy is concerned. Gandhiji's comment on this Upaniṣad is noteworthy. He is of the opinion that if all the Upaniṣads and all other scriptures all on a sudden happened to be reduced to ashes and if only the first verse of the *Īśāvāsyasyopaniṣad* were left in the memory of the Hindus, Hinduism would live forever. He took the three opening words of the *Īśāvāsyasyopaniṣad*: *tena tyaktena bhuñjīthā*, as his *mahāvākya*.

The unusually dense and suggestive language, combining mythological imagery with advanced mystical concepts, is a challenge for unveiling the inner meanings of the *Īśāvāsya mantras*. Each *mantra* of this text has been subjected to different interpretations. There are several Sanskrit commentaries among which that of Śaṅkara and Uvaṭācārya are most prominent. Commentaries, translations and studies written by modern scholars are also popular. Still, even now, this text remains mysterious in its content. It is in this context that the commentary of Muni Narayana Prasad on the *Īśāvāsya Upaniṣad* becomes relevant and important. Swami Muni Narayana Prasad is the present Guru and head of Narayana Gurukula Foundation, founded by Nataraja Guru, the prime disciple and interpreter of Narayana Guru. The main intention of the Gurukula Foundation is to give a global perception to the visions of Narayana Guru, who revisualized Advaita as a living philosophy combining service and duty, based on the concept of one caste, one race, one religion and one God for mankind. As a disciple of Nataraja Guru and Guru Nitya Chaitanya Yati, Muni Narayana Prasad is also continuing this mission. As a part of this mission, he has authored around seventy books in Malayalam and has commented upon the ten principal Upaniṣads, except the *Bṛhadāraṇyaka Upaniṣad*. He states that he wrote these commentaries with a purpose of interpreting them in a new way which enables the reader to have a fresh look at the Upaniṣads befitting the modern age. This is true in the case of his commentry on the *Īśāvāsyopaniṣad* also. The deviation from the line of thought of Śaṅkara and his successive commentators is the most distinct feature of the interpretation of Muni Narayana Prasad. In the context of the explanation of the 15th *mantra* of the *Īśāvāsyopaniṣad* he states:

> The *Upaniṣad* has so far been trying to develop systematically a line of thought by which the core teaching of *brahma-vidyā* (Science of the Absolute) could be revealed. And the way of giving expression to the inexpressible, by resorting to the dialectical method or *yoga buddhi*, has just been delineated.
>
> – Muni Narayana Prasad 2009: 54-55

This is a torchlight for those who enter into the ideals of the interpretation presented by Muni Narayana Prasad.

Like Śaṅkara, Muni Narayana Prasad also uses etymology, but somewhat differently from Śaṅkara, as an effective tool for interpretation. In several contexts, by analysing the literal meaning of the words he discloses the inner ideas of the *mantra*s.

For clarifying dense and complex ideas, he sometimes follows the epistemological ideals of Narayana Guru and quotes passages from his Vedāntic texts like *Darśanamāla* and *Brahmavidyāpañcakaṁ*.

As a follower of Narayana Guru who re-visualized Advaita as a living philosophy, the interpretation of Muni Narayana Prasad is based on the main perspective of neo-Vedānta or practical Vedānta envisaged by Vivekananda, etc.

In this paper these points are presented quoting some examples from the commentary on the *Īśāvāsyopaniṣad* by Muni Narayana Prasad.

The first *mantra*,

īśāvāsyamidaṁ sarvaṁ yatkiñca jagatyāṃ jagat ।
tena tyaktena bhuñjīthā mā gṛdhaḥ kasya svid dhanam ।।

is about *nivṛtti-mārga* or *jñāna-yoga*.

The second *mantra*

kurvanneveha karmāṇi jijīviṣecchataṁ samāḥ ।
evaṁ tvayi nānyatheto 'sti na karma lipyate nare ।।

informs about *pravṛtti-mārga* or *karma-yoga*. According to Śaṅkara, the meaning of the word *bhuñjīthā* in the first verse is *pālayethā* that means "protect yourself". So he states that a person who gains the ultimate knowledge that all the world is enveloped by God should protect the self by giving up all the worldly desires. Such a person, says Śaṅkara, is not eligible for performing *karma* any more or he will withdraw from doing *karma* (*evaṁ īśvarātmabhāvanayā yuktasya putrādyeṣaṇātrayasaṁnyāse eva adhikāraḥ*). The second *mantra*, Śaṅkara argues, is addressed to those who are not competent to know the Self and who are called upon to perform works enjoined in the Vedas. Thus, he makes out the distinction that the way of knowledge is for *saṁnyāsin*s and the way of action is for others. According to him, the way of knowledge and the way of action are contradictory (*jñānakarmaṇoḥ virodhaṁ parvatavat akampyaṁ*).

Muni Narayana Prasad, like several modern thinkers, takes the second *mantra* as a continuation of the first. His interpretation of the passage *tyaktena bhuñjīthā* deserves special attention here. He translates it as "enjoy through renouncing" and gives a detailed explanation on the Upaniṣadic way of enjoying through renouncing. He elucidates that one who realizes the truth that *Īśa* is the Ultimate Reality, underlying all apparent forms, can also recognize all enjoyable objects and their enjoyers belong to *Īśa*. Thus, he realizes that he possesses nothing. On knowing this, he can give up what he thought of as his own. The author concludes:

> In short, first we renounce ourselves and our possessions to their real possessor *Īśa* and then we enjoy what is rightful to us as a part of the total system of life. This is the Upaniṣadic way of enjoying through renouncing.

Quoting passages from *Darśanamālā* and *Brahmavidyā-pañcakaṁ* of Narayana Guru, Muni Narayana Prasad elucidates how a person in this world engaged in actions can live fully liberated or with no *karma* clinging to him. Guru says that it is *Ātman* or *Brahman* itself that performs all the *karma*s:

> *ātmaiva māyayā karma karoti bahurūpadhṛk* ।
>
> – *Darśanamālā*, Karma-Darśana, v. 1

Those, who realize the truth that the *karma*s clinging to them are merely superimposed on them because of *ajñāna* and it is *Ātman* or *Brahman* that performs *karma*s, remain liberated even when being engaged in activities. Muni Narayana Prasad explains that this is the hidden meaning of the passage *na karma lipyate nare*. He states that one can remain as a *karma-yogī* only if endowed with wisdom, only if one is a *jñānī* or a *jñāna-yogī*. And a *jñāna-yogī* in the world of here and now can remain only as a *karma-yogī*, because no *jñānī* can exist without *karma*, physical, mental or verbal. Therefore, this second *mantra* could be treated also as a continuation of the first, clarifying how a *jñāna-yogī* actually lives in this world. This interpretation agrees with the basic perspective of neo-

Vedānta or practical Vedānta.

The interpretation of the third stanza

asuryā nāma te lokāḥ andhena tamasāvṛtāḥ ।
tāṁste pretyābhigacchanti ye ke cātmahano janāḥ ।।

is also specially notable. Muni Narayana Prasad gives new and logical explanations for the two terms *asuryā* and *pretya* in this *mantra*. Some modern scholars like Sri Aurobindo accept an alternative reading *asūryā* (without sunlight) for the word *asuryā*. Here the author, like Śaṅkara, accepts the reading *asuryā* (demonic). Nevertheless, his interpretation differs very much from that of Śaṅkara. On the basis of the concept *daivī sampatti* and *āsurī sampatti*, elaborated in the sixteenth chapter of the *Bhagavadgītā*, he explains how the killers of the Self go to the world of demons. His exposition follows thus:

> Those who do not know themselves virtually kill themselves by living in the blinding darkness of ignorance. They, in effect, make their own lives a world of *asurā*s (demons).

The meaning of the word *pretya* is generally given by almost all the ancient and modern commentators as "on departing from this world on death". Muni Narayana Prasad interprets it as "having departed from the world of the real" which, according to him, is more appropriate to the philosophical context of the *Īśāvāsyopaniṣad*.

Scholars call the central section constituting verses 9-14 the crux or famously difficult passage as their meaning is confusing. The first three of these six verses, *mantra*s 9-11, explain how one can cross over death and attain *amṛtatva* by the combined pursuit of *vidyā* and *avidyā*. The second three verses, *mantra*s 12-14, elucidate how the joint worship or understanding of the manifest (*sambhūti*) and the unmanifest (*asambhūti*) helps one attain *amṛtatva,* crossing over death.

It is difficult to understand what is intended by the *ṛṣi* with the three dualities: *vidyā* and *avidyā*, *sambhūti* and *asambhūti*, and *amṛtaṃ* and *mṛtyuḥ* mentioned here. That is why Swami Ranganathananda states that every one of our old commentators has been compelled to give arbitrary meanings to the keywords in the above six verses to make them intelligible (1993: 140). Yet, as mentioned earlier, they do not seem to have done adequate justice to the thought of these verses when viewed in the light of the general theme of this great Upaniṣad or of the Upaniṣads in general.

Muni Narayana Prasad gives a more reasonable interpretation for these verses. By resorting to the epistemological ideals of Narayana Guru, he discloses the hidden idea of these passages that form the core of the Upaniṣad.

The first three of the six verses of the central section read thus:

> *andham tamaḥ praviśanti ye avidyām upāsate* ।
> *tato bhūya iva te tamo ya u vidyāyām ratāḥ* ।।
>
> Into a blinding darkness enter those who adore ignorance (*avidyā*), and more pitch-black, as it were, is the darkness entered by those who delight in knowledge (*vidyā*).
>
> *anyad evāhur vidyayā anyad āhur avidyayā* ।
> *iti śuśruma dhīrānāṁ ye nas tat vicacakṣire* ।।10।।
>
> Distinct indeed, it is said, is the outcome of knowledge (*vidyā*) and distinct the outcome of ignorance (*avidyā*). We have heard thus from the wise ones who have explained these to us.

vidyāṁ cāvidyāṁ ca yas tad vedobhayaṁ saha ।
avidyayā mṛtyuṁ tīrtvā vidyaya amṛtam aśnute ॥11॥

Knowledge and ignorance, he, who understands these two together, crosses death through ignorance and enjoys immortality through knowledge.

According to Śaṅkara, here *vidyā* is knowledge of deities and *avidyā* is *karma* (*vidyāṁ ca avidyāṁ ca devatājñānaṁ karma ca*). But Muni Narayana Prasad gives a different interpretation to these two terms which seems to be more logical as far as the general theme of the Upaniṣad is concerned. In order to make clear what is meant by *vidyā* and *avidyā*, he quotes the definition of these terms from *Darśanamālā* of Narayana Guru stating that a clear definition of these two core terms of Vedānta is not available in any texts of Vedānta and traditional commentaries. Guru defines them as follows:

anātmā na sad ātmā sad iti vidyotate yayā ।
sā vidyeyaṁyathā rajju-sarpatatvāvadharaṇam ॥
– *Darśanamālā*, Māyādarśanam, v. 3

That because of which the non-Self (*anātmā*) is understood as unreal and the Self as real (*ātmā*) is what this *vidyā* is, as in the case of asserting that the snake is unreal and the rope alone is real.

ātmā na sad anātmā sad iti vidyotate yayā
saivāvidyā yayā rajju-sarpayoḥ ayathārthadṛk
– *Darśanamālā*, Māyādarśanam, v. 4

That because of which the Self (*ātmā*) is understood as unreal, and the non-Self as real (*anātmā*) is what this *avidyā* is, as in the case of wrongly seeing the rope as unreal and the snake as real.

According to the definition of *vidyā* given above, it enables one to understand that *ātman* alone is real and this understanding leads one to brightness. This can never be an experience of darkness. So the statement that darkness covers those who delight in knowledge (*vidyā*) (*tato bhūya iva te tamo ya u vidyāyām ratāḥ*) seems to be a paradoxical one.

Here, Muni Narayana Prasad gives a clear and convincing interpretation to this passage. He explains that the real understanding of *vidyā* leads one to the experience one's own mergence into the being of *ātman* where no enjoyer–enjoyed duality is relevant. But as long as one enjoys *vidyā* and thinks I am a man of wisdom or I am delighted on being a *jñānin* (*vidyāyām ṛtāḥ*) his enjoyerhood, that means I-sense, predominates. That state of mind distances one from the real spirit of wisdom. He summarizes the central idea of the 9th *mantra* thus:

> It would sometimes be possible to save one caught in *avidyā* by proper guidance. But the case of one who enjoys *vidyā* is different. Being a person proud of having gained wisdom, being proud of considering himself as *jñānin*, he can never be saved from the darkness he is in. That darkness, thus, is more pitch-black. – 2009: 40

The second three of the six verses are thus:

> *andhaṁ tamaḥ praviśanti ye asaṁbhūtimupāsate* ।
> *tato bhūya iva te tamo ya u saṁbhūtyāṁ ratāḥ* ।।12।।
>
> Into a blinding darkness enter those who adore non-becoming (*asambhūti*) and more pitch-black, as it were, is the darkness entered by those who delight in creative becoming.
>
> *anyadevāhuḥ saṁbhavāt anyadāhurasaṁbhavāt* ।
> *iti śuśruma dhīrāṇāṁ ye nastat vicacakṣire* ।।13।।

> Distinct indeed, it is said, is the outcome of creative becoming (*sambhava*) and distinct the outcome of non-becoming (*asambhava*). We have heard thus from the wise ones who have explained these to us.
>
> *saṁbhūtiṁ ca vināśaṁ ca yastad vedobhayaṁ saha* ।
> *vināśena mr̥tyuṁ tīrtvā sambhūtyā 'mr̥tamaśnute* ।।14।।
>
> Creative becoming (*sambhūti*) and Destruction (*vināśa*), he who understands these two together, crosses death through ignorance and enjoys immortality through knowledge.

The two terms, *sambhūti* and *asambhūti*, mentioned in the above verses are interpreted by commentators in different ways. According to Śaṅkara, *samabhūti* is *kāryabrahma* called *Hiraṇya-garbha,* that means the manifested. *Asamabhūti* is the unmanifested called by such names as *prakr̥ti*, *kāraṇaṃ* and *avidyā* (*asambhūtiḥ prakr̥tiḥ kāraṇaṁ avidyā*). Swami Ranganathananda understands *sambhūti* as pure being or *Brahman* and *asambhūti* as the world of becoming. Muni Narayana Prasad understands these words in a different sense. According to him *asambhūti* is non-becoming and *sambhūti* is creative becoming. They mark the beginning and end of the phenomenal existence of individual entities, as well as the world. Thus, he explains that those who adore *asaṁbhūti*, that means, those who consider phenomenal appearances as real, are ignorant and they live in worry about death. Those who thus meditate on death or destruction all through life live constantly in a dark world of blinding ignorance. Those who delight in *sambhūti*, creative becoming, think that attaining a state without death, though not at all possible, is the happiest of all events. They live in a darkness more blinding than those who are fearful of death.

After presenting the detailed exposition of these six *mantra*s, the commentator points out their indecipherability and states:

> What is really meant to be conveyed, thus, is not clearly expressed in these words of the *Upaniṣad*. Being ineffable, it is left to the seeker to meditatively visualize on his own. Such is the dialectical methodology adopted in the present *Upaniṣad*. – 2009: 52

However, he concludes that the *vidyā–avidyā* duality pertains to the realm of knowing, one of the functions of the *cit* aspect of *ātman* and the *sambhūti–asambhūti* duality comes within the context of the manifestation of what really exists, which is the *sat* aspect of *ātman*.

According to the traditional interpretation, the last portion of the *Īśāvāsyopaniṣad* consisting of *mantra*s 15-18 is the prayer to Pūṣan, the Sun God, by a spiritual seeker at the time of his death. Here also Muni Narayana Prasad gives a new elucidation which, he says, is more appropriate to the core spirit of the *Īśāvāsyopaniṣad*. The first *mantra* in this section follows thus:

> *hiraṇmayena pātreṇa satyasyāpihitaṁ mukham* ।
> *tattvaṁ pūṣannapāvṛṇu satyadharmāya dṛṣṭaye* ॥15॥
>
> The face of Reality is covered over with a golden casket. Uncover it, Oh Pūṣan, so that I, who put the real to practice in life, may behold it.

Here, instead of the conventional meaning of Pūṣan as the Sun God he accepts the derivational meaning *poṣaṇāt pūṣā*, that means "the one who nourishes". Thus, he interprets that here *pūṣā* is *Īśa* or *ātman* as it is the Reality that nourishes every being. And this Reality, conceived here as *pūṣā*, is requested to be gracious enough to open the golden casket and enable one to perceive the real secret of the Upaniṣadic teaching. Again he substantiates all the epithets – *pūṣā*, *ekarṣi*, *yama*, *sūrya* and *prājāpatya* in the next *mantra*, which according to the traditional interpretation address the Sun God – are applicable to *ātman*. As *ātman* is conceived as pure effulgence and being *ānanda* in essence, the following last lines of the sixteenth *mantra* become significant:

> *tejo yatte rūpaṁ kalyāṇatamaṁ tatte paśyāmi* ।
>
> Gather back a portion of your splendid rays so that I may behold the brilliant, auspicious form of yours,

also can be interpreted as a prayer made by the supplicant to the *ātman*.

The last line,

> *yosāvasau puruṣaḥ so 'hamasmi* ।

which means "The unseen universal person (*puruṣa*), that I behold in you – I am He", says Muni Narayana Prasad, is a variant version of the *mahāvākya* – *ahaṁ brahmāsmi* – of Vedānta.

Thus, the interpretation of the *Īśāvāsya mantra*s given by Muni Narayana Prasad enables a reader to have a fresh look at the *Īśāvāsyopaniṣad*. He examines the etymological derivation of words, justifies them based on the ideas of different philosophical texts and relates them to the core idea of the text. Interpreting the *mantra*s in such away, he follows the Advaita doctrine of Narayana Guru, who in real sense is a *jñāna-yogī* and a *karma-yogī*, whose Advaita is combined with service and duty.

References

Azikkot, Sukumar, 2001, *Tattvamasi*, Kottayam: D.C. Books.

Eswaran, Ekanath, 2011, *The Upaniṣads*, Mumbai: Jaico Publishing House.

Hume, Robert Ernest, 1993, *The Thirteen Principal Upanisads,* Delhi: Oxford University Press.

Īśāvāśyopaniṣad with the *Bhāṣya* of Śaṅkara (with *Ṭīkā* of Ānandagiri), *Bhāṣya* of Uvaṭācārya, *Īśāvāsyarahasyam* of Brahmānanda, *Īśāvāsyadīpikā* by Śaṅkarānanda, *Īśāvāsyavivṛti* by Rāmacandra Paṇḍita and *Īśāvāsyarahasya* by Ānandabhaṭṭopādhyāya. (Title page of the book that gives editor/publisher/place of publication/year of publication missing.)

Muni Narayana Prasad, 2009, *Īśāvāsya and Muṇḍaka Upanisads*, Translation and Commentary, New Delhi: D.K. Printworld.

Nair, G. Balakrishnan, 2010, *Śrīnārāyaṇaguradevakr̥tikaḷ Sampūrṇavyākhyānam,* vols I-II, Thiruvanantapuram: Kerala Bhasha Institute.

Radhakrishnan, S., 2012, *The Principal Upaniṣads*, Noida: Harper Collins Publishers.

Ranganathananda, Swami, 1993, *The Message of the Upaniṣads,* Bombay: Bharatiya Vidya Bhavan.

Sreedharan, M.K., Swamini Sreedharan, 2008, *Gurudevan*, Thiruvanantapuram: Siso Books.

3

Ontological and Axiological Vision in Brahmavidyāpañcakam

B. Sugeetha

THE genius of Narayana Guru is evident in *Brahmavidyāpañcakam*, a composition which condenses the essential content of the Śāṅkara school of Vedānta in just five verses, thus avoiding unnecessary verbosity. In this short text, the problems which arise when trying to understand *Brahman*, the method adopted to resolve them and the validity of such a method are stated.

The Vedānta introduced by Narayana Guru in this work is not meant for doctrinal understanding alone, but also instructs the student to visualize the manifest Reality as oneself; become fully convinced that the Reality is unconditioned consciousness in essence; and perceive himself/herself as a functional modulation of the same Reality. Understanding that this Reality alone functionally exists, even in the minutest aspects of life, makes one's life an unbroken stream of happiness.

The word *Brahman* (the Absolute), derived from the verb root *bṛḥ* (to grow), signifies the inconceivable, unconditional Reality which unfolds itself incessantly as all conditional forms, both in the conceptual and perceptual worlds. One invisible Reality is poetically imagined as growing into all the multitudinous visible forms. Being Pure Consciousness (*cit*) in essence, it transcends the bounds of all conceptualizations, no matter how great.

In Narayana Guru's work *Arivu* the nature of this consciousness-Reality is depicted thus:

> *The being of consciousness*
> *Is all-inclusive plentitude*
> *Then, where else can exist*
> *Anything that is not Consciousness?* – Verse 4

As consciousness is all-inclusive, the supposed non-consciousness also has its being within consciousness. Thus, nothing exists outside the plentitude of consciousness.

The *Brahmavidyāpañcakam* adopts the format of a dialogue between a *guru* and a *śiṣya*. In the first verse the *śiṣya* raises two fundamental questions which all philosophies seek to answer: "Who am I? (*ko 'ham*?)" and "From where did this world originate? (*kuto jagat*?)".

In the second verse the Guru answers the first question "Who am I?" by stating, "You are *Brahman* indeed". He clarifies further by saying: "You are not the senses (*indriyas*); you are not the mind (*manas*); you are not the intellect (*buddhi*); you are not the storehouse of knowledge (*citta*); you are not the physical body (*vapuḥ*); you are not the functional vitality (*prāṇa*); you are not the I-sense; you are not anything else." He goes on to say that *ātmā* is beyond all these.

Whence then error? The potential in the Lord (*Brahman*) to cause universal error (*māyā*) and individual error (*avidyā*) is beginningless (*anādi*), but is not endless (*ananta*), because it vanishes when one becomes enlightened. Everything is an illusory appearance caused by this *māyā* or *avidyā*, which are at the basis of our wrong understandings, "I am this body", "I am the senses", " I am the *prāṇa*", "I am the mind", "I am knowledge" and the like. All such appearances and notions are unreal (*asat*) and are superimposed on *ātmā*. They are to be understood as *anātmā* (non-self). *Anātmā*, thus, is the dialectical counterpart of *ātmā*.

The world does not and cannot have an existence of its own. Its appearance is like that of water in a mirage. This truth is to be properly and intensely perceived by the *śiṣya*. The perceiver of this Reality sees oneself in all the beings and all the beings in oneself. Verse 6 of the *Īśa Upaniṣad* also indicates this.

The Axiological Vision

Guru's direct answer *tvam hi brahma* pacifies the disciple to a great extent. He/she is immediately free of all fears concerning life and its problems. One in fear cannot be taught properly. Fear arises from the notion that "I" the person who fears is different from the world that makes "me" frightened. This notion is rooted out by the assuring words "You are *Brahman* indeed". The individual being does not exist separate from the total being signified by the word *Brahman*. This answers the second question, "From where did this world originate?" We have seen that one who perceives this Reality sees oneself in all the beings and all beings in oneself. With this assurance gained, one's inner agony as well as one's confused state of mind become calm.

As we have seen, the word *Brahman* signifies the one all-pervading Reality that assumes the form of everything physical and mental. *Brahman* is one substance ceaselessly assuming new forms which eventually face destruction only to be replaced by newer ones. *Brahman* as substance is understood as *sat* (existence). This substance being consciousness in essence is thought of as *cit* (consciousness). The ultimate benefit of realizing this Reality is gaining supreme happiness (*ānanda*) and absolute freedom, experienced in consciousness (*cit*) as existing (*sat*).

The first question "Who am I?" arises when Reality is seen from the subjective perspective. The second question, "From where did this world originate?" arises from the objective perspective. Reality is neither subjective nor objective, and therefore not an object to be known. All forms of objective knowledge have an implied subject–object duality. But realizing *Brahman* is not a knowledge of *Brahman* as an object that can be known. It is the experiential awareness of the subject becoming fully merged in the reality of *Brahman*, and realizing *Brahman* as the being of oneself or Self (*ātmā*). Thus, *Brahman* is *ātmā*, and *ātmā* is *Brahman*. This dialectical unity is implicit in the dictum, *tvam hi brahma*.

Our direct experience of ourself or the existence of the world is not divided into mind or matter. These dual notions arise only when we think about our experience. These dualities are mere constraints of our intellect. The intellect, in the context of the search for Reality, is merely a minute functional mode of what we are searching for. This is why the seers repeatedly remind us that the Ultimate Reality is incomprehensible by the intellect. The way to transcend this duality is by dialectical methodology which transcends logical reasoning. It is portrayed by Narayana Guru in *Ātmopadeśa Śatakam*, verse 74:

Countless are the particles of dust
That constitute the earth;
And the earth that exists in and through the particles
Has no different being either
Likewise, matter merges in the being of mind,
And mind in the material bodies.
The two thus become revealed to be
One in essence when contemplatively perceived.

Thus, the Guru teaches the disciple "You are the Reality beyond the duality of mind and matter". *Ātmā* and *Brahman* are inseparably one Existence in essence (*sat*), one Consciousness in essence (*cit*) and one Value experience is essence (*ānanda*).

Brahman being *sat* in essence, it is the substance that pervades the being of both the knower and the known. What we call *jagat* is the flow of forms assumed by the one *Brahman* through its creative self-manifestation. Vedānta perceives everything – from the distant galaxies to the human brain – as the manifestation of one ontological reality and inseparable from that substance or *Brahman*.

If we begin our search for Reality by accepting creation, sustenance and dissolution as real, the only stand we can take is that everything was born of the one causal Reality, everything has its being in that Reality and everything merges back into that Reality at the time of dissolution. This is comparable to pots, jugs, plates and the like being born of earth, having their being in earth and finally disintegrating into the earth.

The third verse perceives everything as *sat* (existence). The same *sat* in essence is seen as unconditional consciousness (*pratipat*) in the fourth verse. It is easy to conceive a substance underlying the being of everything living and non-living, but how does this substance function consciously to manifest itself as a well-structured world? How do different functions take place in human beings in different states of waking, dreaming and deep sleep? The answer to both these questions is that the existing Reality (*sat*) is pure and unconditional consciousness, called *pratipat* or *cit* in Sanskrit. It is this *pratipat* that functions consciously everywhere. The fourth verse ends with the Master's instructions to the disciple, "You are that *pratipadā* or *cit* or consciousness". This *pratipat* is understood in its conditioned form as causes and effects. Even the zest to know the Real is none other than a minute element of the manifest form of the very same Reality or *pratipat* one is in search of. Thus, the *guru* teaches the disciple the non-duality of the individuated selves and *Brahman* or of the knowing consciousness and the known consciousness: *brahmātmaikya.*

Axiology

The fifth and last verse says:

With a properly calmed mind resulting from
The dawning of Brahman-*wisdom*
You may move around properly in all specific ways,
Joyfully singing, "Pure consciousness indeed I am",
"You (also) are That",
This ātmā *is indeed that* Brahman,
How could there be for you then the bondage of karmas,
Whether already begun (prārabdha),
Accumulated from the past (sañcita),
Or those yet to be accumulated (āgāmī)

Karma is itself unreal.
All such therefore are simply conditionings,
Superimposed on the ātmā *that you really are,*
You really are vibhu *(the one Lord in whom abide all becomings),*
In essence sat–cit, *alone!*

In the second verse, *Brahman* was pictured as the underlying substance in one's own being. The third verse emphasized the *sat* (existence) aspect of *Brahman.* In the fourth verse, the *cit* or *pratipat* (consciousness) aspect was underscored. In the concluding verse, the same *Brahman* is portrayed by Narayana Guru as the realized Reality and supreme happiness of the disciple. Along with it Guru lays bare the inner secrets of the *mahāvākya*s, which enclose within them the core of Vedāṇtic wisdom.

Realizing that all *karma*s are not real, one becomes released from the bondages caused by them. Realizing one's identity with the Ultimate Reality that underlies the being of everything, leads one to the ultimate limit of happiness.

The *mahāvākya – tat tvamasi* – is an instruction given by the *guru* to his disciple, and hence is known as *upadeśa-vākya.*

The disciple upon hearing the instructions sits alone and contemplates and meditates *ayam ātmā brahma* (my Self is *Brahman*). For this reason, this dictum is considered *manana-vākya.* By this contemplation and meditation one attains fulfilment in the realization, *aham brahma asmi*, and hence this dictum is termed *sākṣāt karma kāvya.* The essential content of this realization is made clear in the dictum *prajñānam brahma* (*Brahman* is consciousness), known as *svarūpa-vākya.*

According to the Upaniṣadic ṛsis (seers), Vedānta teaches the oneness in essential content of both the individuated self and the Universal Self, whether conceived as first person, second person, third person, or as impersonal. They have a common content and in that content, which is unconditional consciousness, the individual and the universal find their oneness. This oneness is not merely an intellectual understanding, but is the direct experience of one's own oneness with the one Reality. This experience transforms an individual's life into that of *Brahman* or *sat–cit–ānanda* in essence. One's own life is thus experienced as an everlasting *sat–cit–ānanda* song, as evident from the *guru*'s words asking the disciple to move around properly in all specific ways joyfully singing *prajñānam tu aham asmi* (Pure Consciousness, indeed I am).

What appears as the world is the constantly changing manifest forms of *ātmā*, the real content in oneself. This process of self-unfoldment of *ātmā* happens because of the infinite creative urge inherent in *ātmā* and finds expression as everything, both pleasant and unpleasant, both good and evil, both *dharma* (righteousness) and *adharma* (unrighteousness). All these dualities happen in life and the world as part of *ātmā*'s sportive self-unfoldment. This knowledge enables one to treat both happiness and suffering with a state of equanimity, and equalize both pleasure and pain. This brings a sense of peacefulness and life becomes a constant flow of unconditional happiness (*paramānanda*). The intuitive awareness of the oneness of *ātmā* and the world, where pleasure and pain are equalized, releases us from the realm of relativism and leads us to Absolutism.

സാരഥി
KUWAIT

Contemplative Devotion

4

Swami Tanmaya

> Some instruction has to be given because positive knowledge cannot come by itself. A teacher's authority is involved here. To know, on the contrary, that all beings love happiness, does not require proof or teaching. It is a matter of general observation.
>
> – *Integrated Science of the Absolute*, vol. II, p. 315

Bhakti as Contemplation

NATARAJA Guru, in his translation and commentary on *Darśanamālā*, calls *Bhakti Darśana* (*Vision* by *Contemplation*), translating, in this context, *bhakti* as contemplation. Much like the *Bhagavadgītā*, which emphasizes contemplation in its discussion of *bhakti*, Narayana Guru's discussion of *bhakti* also prizes contemplation over devotion. The *Gītā*, being a revaluation of both orthodox and heterodox tendencies in spirituality, while covering both rational and emotional aspects, has to make clear the role of devotion in the spiritual progress of the aspirant to wisdom. Furthermore, the variety of bipolar relationships of devotion, polytheistic or monotheistic, in the *Gītā* conforms more to a contemplative discipline rather than religious worship. Contemplation seems to fit more to the type of spirituality of the person implied in verses 13-19 of the twelfth chapter of the *Bhagavadgītā*.

The first three verses of *Bhakti Darśana* describe three kinds of meditation that once again lend themselves to a contemplative. In verse 1, *ātmā-anusandhānam,* otherwise known as meditation on the Self, is contemplation. In verse 2, *sadā-brahma-anusandhānam* (constant meditation on the Absolute) is contemplation. Finally, in verse 3, *ānanda-param dhyānam,* (meditation as pertaining to bliss or absolute value) is also contemplation. These types of meditation which involve deep reflective thought of the Absolute will lead one to the inner silence described by all religions.

Narayana Guru wholly accepts the *Bhagavadgītā* view. In Narayana Guru's commentary on the opening verse of the "Bhakti Darśana" of *Darśanamālā,* when a person is fully absorbed in the joy of Self-contemplation he/she has nothing left to seek. Self-bliss is *bhakti* and needs no outward expression of behaviour. The verse 17 of chapter 3 of the *Bhagavadgītā* says:

But for him who happens to be attached to the Self alone,
Who finds full satisfaction in the Self
For such a man who is happy in the Self as such, too,
There is nothing that he should do.

With reference to the *ātmavit* (a knower of the Self) in the first verse of "Bhakti Darśana" *Darśanamālā* demonstrates that wisdom is more important to Narayana Guru's concept of *bhakti* than religious devotion:

Meditation on the Self is contemplation

Because the Self consists of bliss.
A knower of the Self, meditates by the Self
Upon the Self forever.

It is the Self itself that contemplates the Self and not any other deity or divinity of a lower status than the Absolute. The Absolute includes God and the Self without omitting cosmological implications. These implications are part and parcel of the notion of God as it has grown out of Vedism where sacrifices were offered to hypostatic principles representing phenomenal aspects of nature. These principles are deities like Indra, Varuṇa and Agni. It was only later that they were formed into one God called *sarve-devāḥ* (all gods). This single God sprang up under various names such as Karmanaspati (Lord of All Action), Aditi (Mother of Sun-God), Bṛhaspati (Great Lord), Vācaspati (Lord of the Word) and Bṛhamaṇaspati (Lord of the Great Principle).

Hierophantic Presences and Hypostatic Ideals

In making scholarly attempts to synthetically understand these two concepts, it is possible for the mind to get lost in endless hypostatic fixations or hierophantic idolatries if one starts with an asymmetric conception of reality that is in favour of these two extreme normative psychological fixations.

For instance, favouring the hypostatic generates unbalanced stress in the form of innumerable beings such as angels and spirits, whereas emphasizing the hierophantic counter extreme, allows one to attribute inordinate value, to stone images surviving from prehistoric times. These value-results can be good, bad or indifferent depending on how they are treated or permitted to influence human relations or conduct. Inevitably, they find a place, refined or etherealized though they may be, even in the most puritanically iconoclastic or "imageless" religions.

All hypostatic, or "other-wordly", forms have to first be reduced to terms of everyday values in human life, while hierophantic presences, animistically or otherwise conceived, have to be referred to the common norm of the Absolute, before these two can be properly assessed or related in the contemplative context of spiritual progress (Nataraja Guru 2003: 68).

Iconology in India becomes as important as theology in the West. In its own way, it speaks the profound and secret language of dialectics. Although the simple *Śivaliṅgam,* or mark, is just a round upright stone which is decorated and anointed, it becomes an eloquent presence, an inspiring noumenal hierophany. One of the features of this word – iconography – on Indian soil is its synthesis of both doctrine and sacred presence, both the teaching and the numinous feeling. The symbolic icon belongs to language, but it is merely matter when considered as an object, simply stone, wood, metal, paper, etc. But not even the simplest idolaters in India take the idol to be "just matter". It speaks to them, however vague or crude it may be. The dumb stones require a traditionally trained or dialectically contemplative ear attuned to the message of their secret sermon (ibid.: 157-58).[1]

All religions have underlying hierophantic presences and hypostatic ideals, which are revalued by Narayana Guru at length. Śiva culture and Upaniṣadic culture are given their due places in his vision of one religion for mankind. It is in verse 13 of *Ātmopadeśa Śatakam* that one sees a mention of Śiva:

---

[1] Nataraja Guru, 2003, *The Word of the Guru*, Delhi: D.K. Printworld.

Unto the Master who dons the ashes of the three modes,
Offering the flower of inner self, inclining before Him,
With all sense interests effaced, divest of all and cool,
Even from the grandeur of loneliness bereft, into glory sink.

Next, in verse 14, it asks us to remember the Upaniṣadic secret lore:

That light, rid of threefold view, that ever brighter burns
Upsurging and brim-full beyond the bounds of the triple worlds,
Remember, it will never come within the reach
Of a hermit untrue, as Upaniṣadic secret lore declares.

Idolatry and hierophantic presences are dominant in Śiva culture, while Vedic culture and Semitic religions are rich in hypostatic ideals. According to B. Karunakaran:

> The flow of the vision of Narayana Guru is as a confection of Vaidika Advaita (Vedānta) and Āgama Advaita (Śiva *tattva*). – 2018: 163

Another scholar V.K. Hariharan Unnithan states:

> Śāṅkara Advaita is helping the contemplative make non-dual thinking, the subject for unitive understanding and then recedes to inner silence. At the same time, Śaiva Advaita takes this non-dual consciousness to an imperiential transcendence (*anubhūti*). – 2019: 34

One Religion for Mankind

It is even bliss that all do meditate,
No one at all (meditates) suffering.
That which is meditation of bliss,
As contemplation it is taught. – Bhakti Darśana, verse 3

In this verse, Narayana Guru underlines a truth which is both a secret of secrets, as well as an overtly acceptable universal characteristic of life. The key to a universal religion sets happiness as the goal for all living creatures. This is the basis of the "one religion" that he always stood for.

Guru has stated in verse 49 of *Ātmopadeśa Śatakam*:

Every man at every time makes effort in every way
Aiming at his self-happiness; therefore in this world
Know faith as one; understanding thus,
Shunning evil, the inner self into calmness merges.

The Guru not only presents the happy prospect of "One Religion" for all mankind in a scientific and public sense, but more pointedly, that each person has to adopt this attitude to find peace of mind and attain happiness for himself/herself.

Sensuous Joy Is Not Sin

Pleasure derived from sense objects is really just pleasure by the Self alone. The ignorant man considers pleasure to be existing in things and is thus attracted to them. But the wise man finds pleasure in himself, and sees the universality of such a pleasure. The well-known instance of the dialogue between Yājñavalkya and his wife Maitreyī in *Bṛhadāraṇyaka Upaniṣad* IV.5.1ff. supports this point.

The wife does not merely adore the husband,
Nor the husband merely adore the wife;
It is Self-bliss alone that they adore
As lodged within every sensuous object.
– *Bhakti Darśana*, verse 7

The inclusion of sensuous joy, which is often treated as "sin" by certain religions, is scientifically examined here by Narayana Guru. This should not be interpreted to mean that sensuousness or sin is condemned, but that Narayana Guru is more interested in revealing the content of the Absolute sincere and wholehearted secret of wisdom. There are also verses in the *Bhagavadgītā* supporting this position.

There are numerous verses in the *Bhagavadgītā*, for example, X.28 and X.36, where the Absolute is described as both god of erotics (*kandarpaḥ*) and the chance-risk behind gambling. Sin is a horizontal factor and as such is outside the scope of contemplation.

In *Bhagavadgītā* X.28, we read:

Of weapons I am the thunderbolt;
of cows I am the milk-yielder of all desires;
of progenitors I am the god of erotics;
of serpents I am Vāsuki (their chief).

In *Bhagavadgītā* X.36, we read:

I am the chance-risk of (*irresponsible*) *gamblers;*
I am the brilliance of brilliant (*people*);
I am victory; I am decisiveness;
I am the goodness of those established in the real.

Absolute and Compassion

We read in *Ātmopadeśa Śatakam* 67:

That which is beyond count on the one hand
And what is ordinary and of the work a day world;
Other than these two, there is no other form at all
Either in memory, in sleep, or in the city on high.

There are two archetypes of knowledge to which all reality may be said to belong without exception or remainder. The first, mentioned in the verse above, is the Absolute as conceived in the present connotation which is beyond all plurality. The Absolute, which is represented vertically and attaining inner silence, can be conceptual or perceptual. The other archetype of knowledge being ordinary or actual is expressed as compassion. These components have to be put together for us to arrive at the normative notion of the Absolute.

Human values are lodged in the human personality. Each human life is to be understood in terms of the fusion and coalescence of two fundamental regulators, the unifying common kindliness in personal relations, i.e. compassion, and the unitive supreme value, Absolute. These two levels or extremes, the outspreading world of kindliness and the Absolute, are indicated as value-emerging factors. But here kindliness draws its meaning from the Absolute, while the Absolute itself becomes meaningless and insipid unless thought of in terms of "the good" or "the generous". Contemplation alone can annul the distinction between these seemingly dual value constituents. Through contemplation these distinctions vanish once the inner silence is attained.

Inner Silence

The history of Vedic thought passes through the stages of Saṁhitās (compendiums of Vedic thought), Brāhmaṇas (literature treatments of the Absolute), Āraṇyakas (philosophical forest treatises) and, finally, the Upaniṣads, where the psychological and cosmological fully blend in the Self. Even in the Upaniṣads, the ideas of *Brahman, ātmā* and *ānanda* are often used interchangeably. It is the novel fusion of these three distinct concepts that Narayana Guru explores in the "Bhakti Darśana", verse 2:

The Absolute is meditated upon
Because it consists of bliss.
Constant meditation on the Absolute
Is thus known as contemplation.

The Absolute's value is implied in the common reference of both *ānanda* and *Brahman*, since both are made up of the stuff of essential value. The term *sadā* (constant or always) underlies the principle of continuity that forms the essence of contemplation. Interrupted or piecemeal contemplation does not have a real or cumulative effect. It has to be constant and of a bipolar nature.

Conclusion

It was the secret of stillness, silence or neutrality, which Narayana Guru possessed in rare abundance, that made him the source of energy: physical, mental and spiritual. It was the secret of such a stillness that made him the most successful educator and helper of men. This was the secret that made him the Guru. The essence of all religion is also one that can be expressed in these three words: silence, stillness and neutrality.

References

Hariharan Unnithan, V.K., 2019, *Ātmopadeśa Śatakam Laghuvṛtti,* (Malayalam and Hindi), Edappal: Vallathol Vidyapeetham.

Karunakaran, B., 2018, *Sri Sankarente Vaidika Advaitavum Sri Narayanante Matatita Advaitavum* (Malayalam), Kollam: Manjari Publications.

Nataraja Guru, 2003, *The Word of the Guru*, Delhi: D.K. Printworld.

———, 2020, *An Integrated Science of the Absolute,* vol. 2, New Delhi: D.K. Printworld.

5

Nataraja Guru

S. Omana

NATARAJA Guru's guruhood is pure and philosophically correct, making as few concessions as possible to relativistic or social notions. He is a Guru of Absolutist truth. His is not the popular conception of an Upaniṣadic or āśramic pattern. It is a new form of guruhood for a truly global world. Narayana Guru did the initial spadework by breaking through the fixed Indian orthodox pattern, as far as he was able to in his own lifetime, without destroying the cultural background. His work was experimental and his success showed the way to his beloved disciple Nataraja Guru to plunge ahead on a wider and entirely universal scale. Nataraja Guru, therefore, has grafted guruhood on to a global background.

Nataraja Guru (1895-1973) was the youngest, yet the foremost among the disciples of Narayana Guru. He was a great scholar who fully imbibed the visions of Narayana Guru and highlighted the words of the Guru in such a way as to reach one and all. Thus, the radiance of Narayana Guru's words spread throughout the world. Natarajan became a Guru by virtue of his spiritual loyalty and by the right of inheritance in order to highlight the philosophical messages of his own great master, Narayana Guru. According to John Spiers, a Westerner and the first disciple of

Nataraja Guru, Narayana Guru was the leading *ṛsi* and scientist as far as Nataraja Guru was concerned. Guru's vision was spiritual and at the same time amenable to scientific poof. Nataraja Guru presented Narayana Guru's vision in a way which could be approved both spiritually and scientifically. By comparing Guru's vision with the philosophical thoughts of the West he emphasized its integrity and scientific nature. Thus, he renewed the value of the Guru's visions by assimilating them to the needs of the present world and thus making it acceptable to the present generation.

Narayana Guru was not confined to the narrow walls of any religion or region but always thought of a world without any boundaries. The Western world came to know of Narayana Guru through Nataraja Guru who installed the vision of a unitive world as envisaged by Narayana Guru in the hearts and minds of people by his everyday life, his works and his institutions relentlessly. During his lifetime, he highlighted the unity of such a world in different fields like knowledge outlook, education, brotherhood, wealth and beauty. He wrote many books with a view to prepare a rough sketch for all these notions.

Nataraja Guru (Natarajan) was born as the second son of Dr Palpu and Bhagavathy on 18 February 1895 in Mysore. He had the great fortune to have a father who was devoted to Narayana Guru, even before he was born.

His initiation into studies was at a village school in Thiruvananthapuram and his primary education was in Malayalam and Kannada. He completed his education at the school in Tipu Sultan's palace in Bangalore, St. Joseph's Thiruvananthapuram, Maharaja's School, Trinity College, Ceylon (Sri Lanka), Presidency College, Madras and so on. He graduated in 1919, majoring in English literature with two science subjects, Zoology (main) and Geology (subsidiary). In 1922, he passed MA and LT together.

He had an innate interest in spirituality and was very much drawn to the discourses of learned *swāmīs*. He became familiar with the *Bhagavadgītā* and Upaniṣads in childhood itself, and memorized the important *ślokas* in them. In his childhood he was very much drawn to Narayana Guru. He was in the habit of reading 100 pages a day. He had an inherent talent in literature, music and painting. He started doing social service while he was a student in school itself.

Natarajan used to meet Narayana Guru frequently in the *āśrama* and also at his father Dr Palpu's home. On one occasion, Guru said: "Doctor I don't have children. You should give me one of yours." The doctor replied: "You can have all my children." Nataraja Guru's curiosity was aroused whenever he met the Guru and he was attracted by the Guru's unusual personality. As time passed, that attraction intensified.

Natarajan returned to his house near Ernakulam railway station after passing MA, LT. As he entered to show his father his LT result, he saw the Guru seated in his father's chair. Again his father offered his children to Guru. After the initial courtesies, the Guru asked for Natarajan's opinion. When Natarajan said that he wanted to live with the Guru forever, Guru was not surprised. The Guru directed him to stay in Advaita Ashram, Aluva. He began life there in August 1922, starting his new life with a silent prayer, dedicating his life for the service of the Guru. There was no special ritual or rite. For sometime, he worked as an English teacher there. Thereafter, he was appointed as Headmaster in Sivagiri School. He approached the Guru alone always and after spending an hour or two, sometimes engaged in a discussion with the Guru. At other times he remained silent with closed eyes. Natarajan's doubts were cleared by a mere look or the silence of the Guru.

"The whole world should become a *gurukulam*" was the blessing given by Narayana Guru. Natarajan dedicated his life towards that goal and with the blessings and best wishes of Narayana Guru, founded a contemplative fraternity in 1923 open to all who seek the wisdom of the Absolute in living terms. In later years Nataraja Guru started many Narayana Gurukula centres in India as well as abroad.

Narayana Guru realized the need to introduce his vision in the language of modern scientific education. He sent his disciple for higher studies to Europe. On arrival there Natarajan joined the fellowship school in Geneva as a physics teacher for five years. He enrolled at the Sorbonne University in Paris, and in 1932 secured DLitt from Sorbonne University with triple Honours. While in Geneva, Natarajan published a series of articles in *Sufi Quarterly.* This invited the attention of many famous Western philosophers like Romain Rolland, Sir Francis Younghusband, etc. Nataraja Guru has written a number of books on Narayana Guru and his philosophy. He also translated most of Narayana Guru's works into English.

The Word of the Guru: This is Nataraja Guru's first book which introduces Narayana Guru as an example of a model *guru*, encompassing both silence and kindness. Part One of the book was written while Narayana Guru was still living.

In 1897 Narayana Guru composed *One Hundred Verses of Self-Instruction* (*Ātmopadeśa Śatakam*), an original Vedānta textbook. Nataraja Guru's commentary has kept in view both Eastern and Western philosophy, giving equal importance to the physical and metaphysical aspects of life. An essential study and analysis of *Ātmopadeśa Śatakam* transforms life into a contemplative prayer leading to peace and happiness. Nataraja Guru used this work as the basis of his *Philosophy of a Guru*.

In 1916 Narayana Guru composed the *Darśanamālā,* representing a high level of mystical literature which became the basis for the amalgamation of all philosophies. Written in traditional Sanskrit and structured as a "garland of visions", the Guru strung together a series of philosophical visions, expressing the same non-dual Truth through ten different points of view. Truth, like an invisible golden thread, reveals itself through each of the hundred *śloka*s.

Nataraja Guru's magnum opus, *An Integrated Science of the Absolute,* is a commentary on the *Darśanamālā.* The work is so structured as to bring together, under a single directive principle, all modern, mythological, Eastern, Western and poetic movements that have taken place in the history of mankind.

Nataraja Guru's translations of the poems of Narayana Guru are found in *An Anthology of the Poems of Narayana Guru*.

Nataraja Guru's interpretation of the *Bhagavadgītā* is a welcome addition to the *Gītā* literature as it brings a freshness of approach to bear on the subject and a critical attitude of mind mellowed by lifelong meditation and wide travel. Nataraja Guru's interpretation highlights Vyasa's philosophical outlook on the *Gītā*.

In order to give a clear picture of Narayana Guru's philosophy, Nataraja Guru has written three series of studies which can be considered as the preface or an annexe of *Ātmopadeśa Śatakam*:

- *The Search for a Norm in Western Thought* – Introduces the leading thinkers of the Western world whose thoughts align with the Yogic way.
- *Vedanta Revalued and Restated* – This is a book written by updating the values of traditional Indian philosophy.
- *The Philosophy of a Guru* – in this book Nataraja Guru uncovers the structural methodology of Narayana Guru's composition and explains the important elements in his philosophic stance and way of interpretation by citing *śloka*s from *Ātmopadeśa Śatakam*.

The "One World" visualized by the Guru is a world of knowledge. In order to introduce Narayana Guru's vision of "One World" to the seekers of Truth, he wrote two books *World Government Memorandum* (*Eka Loka Sarkar*) and World Education Manifesto (*Eka Loka Vidyābhyāsam*).

Nataraja Guru wrote *Towards One World Economics* to explain the need for a Global Economic Policy for a united one world instead of individual policies of each nation.

In his book *Dialectical Methodology,* which includes *Man–Woman Dialectics,* Nataraja Guru has restated Yoga as a modern perennial science of dialectics applicable in all fields. *Wisdom: The Absolute Is Adorable* is a collection of essays, ranging from philosophical notions to social and religious values.

Nataraja Guru's structural analysis and protolinguistic interpretation of the 100 verses of the *Saundarya Laharī* of Śaṅkarācārya establishes the work as a text of Vedānta, rather than a commentary on *Tantra Śāstra.* In his bold attempt to develop a language to unify the thoughts of mankind, Nataraja Guru submitted a monogram to the Royal Academy of Belgium titled, "A Scheme of Integration of Elements of Thought in View of a Language of Unified Science".

In his *Autobiography of an Absolutist,* Nataraja Guru introduces the reader to the path that he walked. When we analyse this book we sense the deep presence of science and philosophy throughout the book. Nataraja Guru intense love for knowledge and the loftiness of the satisfaction of its fulfilment is revealed as a miraculous experience.

The name of Nataraja Guru will be remembered with gratitude, for ever, as the foremost Narayana Guru-philosopher and Absolutist of our time.

References

Nataraja Guru, 1974, *Word of the Guru*, Fernhill: East West University Publication. (D.K. Printworld, New Delhi, 2022).

———, 1977, *An Integrated Science of the Absolute*, 2 vols, Fernhill: East West University. (D.K. Printworld, New Delhi, 2020).

———, 1996, *Experiencing One World*, New Delhi: D.K. Printworld.

———, 2011, *Autobiography of an Absolutist*, New Delhi: D.K. Printworld.

6

In the Stream of Consciousness

Swami Vyasa Prasad

VERSE 79 of *Ātmopadeśa Śatakam* says, *cit prabhāvam ellām,* "All is flux and becoming within the mind-stuff pure". Bergson, the philosopher of flux, was one of the first to illustrate cognition and intuition with the cinematograph which had then just come into vogue. The word translates to "writing in movement". (Greek *kinema* = movement; *grapho* = to write). Greek *kinema* comes from the Proto-Indo-European root *keie* meaning "to set in motion", itself could be from the Sanskrit *cyavate* "stirs himself, goes".

The cinematograph creates an illusion of motion by rapidly projecting a series of static pictures, which the mind fuses together into a seamless experience. Similarly, the mind receives perceptual cues and like a magician creates an experience by clothing perpetual data with conceptual garments. It is possible to study the structure of the psychic dynamism which is normally in perpetual motion. Structural thinking enters modern Western philosophy through the "schema" of Kant. The Rune's dictionary definition is, "The procedure of the imagination by which the categories of the understanding are applied to the manifold of sensuous intuitions". In simpler language, it implies that the mind envisions a gestalt or a pattern. A pattern is an organized structure. A good example of structure is a periodic crystal like salt, which is the repetition of a basic pattern. Living cells, on the other hand, are aperiodic. What mysterious intelligence governs the morphogenesis of an aperiodic crystal like Deoxyribonucleic acid (DNA)? Verse 27 of *Ātmopadeśa Śatakam* says:

Sitting in the dark, that which knows is the Self;
what is known then assumes name and form,
with the psychic dynamism, senses, agency of action and also action;
see how it all comes as mahendra magic!

In the Upaniṣadic context, the second verse of the *Māṇḍūkya Upaniṣad* presents a formula leading to a fourfold structure: Everything is *Brahman* = this *ātman* is *Brahman* = this *ātman* has four parts, *catuṣpāt* (*sarvaṁ hyetad brahma ayamātmā brahma so 'yamātmā catuṣpāt*). This *mantra* also gives us the *mahāvākya, ayamātmā brahma* (This Self is the Absolute). The four limbs are four functional modes of *ātman*: wakeful, dream, deep sleep and the Fourth (*turīya*). Waking, dreaming and deep sleep are conditioned experiences, while *turīya* is transparent consciousness. Narayana Guru defines *turīya* in verse 28 of *Ātmopadeśa Śatakam* as:

Without bottom or top,
from bottom to the crest,
What transparent consciousness has,
that is turīya consciousness.

Turīya consciousness is independent of physiological consciousness and reflex actions which are inhibitory in their effects.

We bring in Euclid at this stage to mark a dimensionless point and draw three concentric circles which represent the basic structure and function of consciousness (*fig*. 6.1). The central locus stands for the alpha point or ground, recognized by Vedāntins as pure beingness of absolute value called *ānanda*. This is the source as well as the final culmination from which a pulsation (*spandana*) arises and eventually gets reabsorbed through centrifugal and centripetal movements. The small circle surrounding the point is the repository of all incipient memories (*vāsanās*). The dreamer, magician and artist arise from here. The second circle represents the threshold of consciousness from where it expands to the frontiers of objectivity. Two ambivalent forces operate here: "hope, love, compassion", and "stifling depression". The outer circle represents

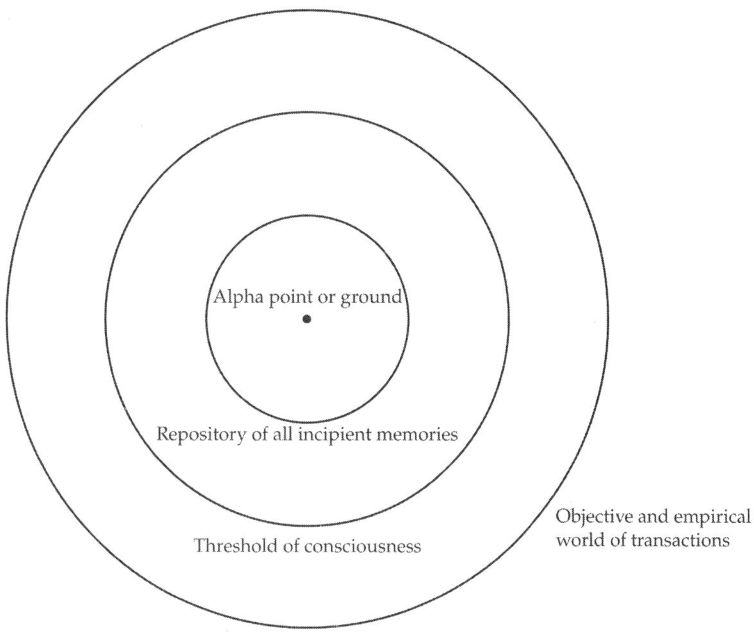

fig. 6.1: Basic structure and function of Consciousness

the objective and empirical world of all our transactions. It is the actual world we see around ourselves, from the pebble under our feet to the distant galaxy.

Much before the invention of the alphabet, human beings communicated using protolinguistic symbols and images. This avoided the verbosity and vagueness of metalanguage, which has become a bane in the modern world. Protolanguage is a very useful tool for translating *lingua mystica* into *lingua scientifique.* Structure and function go together and so understanding the structure of consciousness reveals the function as well. Understanding is the key to transcendence. Though a scientist, Eddington spoke of subjectivism, selectivism and structuralism to draw our attention to the subjective dynamics which structures the world that we seemingly experience "out there".

The alpha point of *fig*. 6.1 is extended vertically to get a parameter from the alpha at the bottom to the omega at the top. Since the visible world is three-dimensional, any point on the circumference of the circle is joined to the centre and to the omega point to create a triangle. By rotating the two-dimensional triangle in space we get a three-dimensional cone. By intersecting the cone with a plane we get sections such as circle, ellipse, parabola and hyperbola. Our auditory experience surrounds us like spherical space. We know that the sun, earth and moon are all spheres. Pythagoras thought of the proportions in their movements in terms of music: the *musica universalis* (music of the spheres). Vision is more cone-like as rays of light converge and pass through the pupil. In the retina, cones are responsible for colour and space acuity. Even communication uses the cone-like megaphone or large terrestrial dishes sending signals to a distant satellite, resembling a radio wave cone. When we think of expressions and impressions, they resemble a cone: a point expanding in time into larger and larger circles of influence, or experiences funnelling into registered impressions in consciousness.

In *fig*. 6.2 two cones are juxtaposed to give a protolinguistic representation of the flux of consciousness as mentioned in the *Māṇḍūkya Upaniṣad.* "The World of Wakeful Consciousness" is *jāgrat;* the "World of Dream Consciousness" is *svapna;* the "World of Incipient Memories" is *suṣupti;* and the base of the upright cone represents the foundation *turīya*. The reality, eternity and "unborn" nature of this ultimate state of consciousness is stated by Gauḍapāda in his *Māṇḍūkya Kārikā* (4.45) as follows:

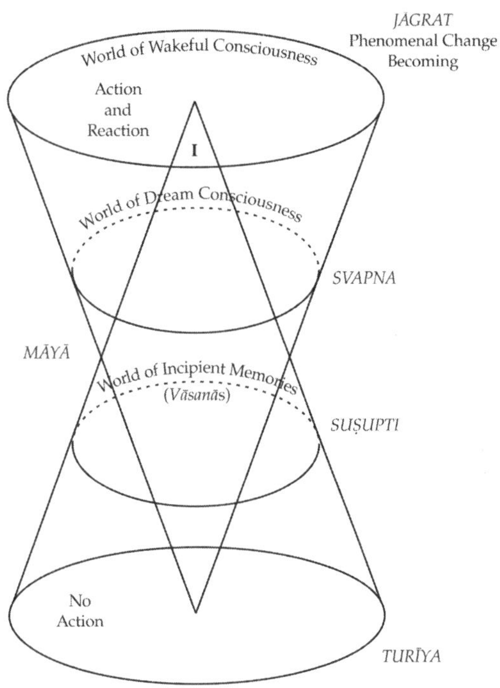

fig. 6.2: Protolinguistic representation of the flux of Consciousness

jātyābhāsaṁ calābhāsaṁ vastvābhāsaṁ tathaiva ca ।
ajācalam avastutvaṁ vijñānaṁ śāntam advayam ।।

Seemingly born, seemingly moving,
as well as seemingly elemental [*in its nature*]
Is this consciousness, which is unborn, immoveable and non-elemental.
[*This consciousness*] *is calm and non-dual.*

A modern poet like Emily Dickinson has similar intuition when she writes:

The Brain is wider than the Sky,
For, put them Side by Side,
The one the other will contain
With ease, and you beside.

Higher consciousness subsumes lower states of consciousness, like Chinese boxes, the smaller ones snuggly fit inside the larger ones.

The cone with the base above represents the inverted world of transactions in which consciousness shrinks to an "I" point of awareness, surrounded by the vast horizontal world of phenomenal change and becoming. Here, a person experiences the *Geworfenheit* (thrownness) of Heidegger. Reciprocally, the vast ever-changing world of wakeful experience spirals inwards to be recorded as memories (*vāsanā*s). Reciprocity unites the two cones. From the unconscious a pulsation initiates the movement of consciousness, like bubbles rising in a liquid, gathering the impressions stored in the *vāsanā*s, to "burst open" and expend their potential energy in the dream and wakeful worlds. Between these two limits, one of continuous change and activity and the other actionless witnessing, the dynamism of *māyā*, along with her handmaids the *vāsanā*s (incipient memories), creates the fantasy world of dream consciousness and the wakeful world of *jāgrat* with infinite variety. Verse 67 of *Ātmopadeśa Śatakam* clearly distinguishes the two aspects of being and becoming, one absolute and the other relative:

> *One is beyond what may be counted,*
> *The other is ordinary; other than these two there is not any other form*
> *Existing in waking, or in dream, or in some city of the gods; this is certain.*

Thus, no matter how alluring and "bright" the wakeful world seems, it is the farthest from the pure state of consciousness. In other words pure consciousness is the weakest in wakeful consciousness and, therefore, Guru says in verse 7 of *Ātmopadeśa Śatakam*, "Do not wake anymore and without sleeping remain as knowledge". The advice is not to get carried away by momentary infatuations at the cost of losing contemplation.

Śaṅkara gives precedence to the cause over the effect (Sat-Kāraṇavāda) and places the entire gamut of gross, subtle and causal interactions in the domain of the unreal superimposition of ignorance on *Brahman*. All seeming movements and changes are *vivarta* (illusory), while the basic substance *cit* never undergoes any change. For a seeker of truth, the first step towards self-discovery begins by turning away from the world of objects, directing the senses inwards (*kannukal añcumullaṭakki*), verticalizing and normalizing the mind by prostrating inwardly to the *karu*, the universal mould, out of which both the subjective and the objective worlds are emanating. In this way, one does not lose ones's ontological foothold while investigating the true nature of existence. When the modulation of discrimination arises, the veil of transient *māyā* is removed and everything dissolves into the unified homogeneous matrix of the *turīya* state which shines like the primal sun (verse 35, *Ātmopadeśa Śatakam*).

7

Education and Self-Realization in the Light of Narayana Guru's Wisdom Teachings

Anjumol V.

SWAMI Vivekananda defines education as "the process by which character is formed, strength of mind is increased and intellect is sharpened, as a result of which one can stand on one's own feet". According to Carl Jung, there is an innate creative spark in every individual, the basis of which lies in the unconscious depths of his mind. So man has a strong innate urge or motive to express his talents or abilities. But if that urge is blocked or deviated in any way, the psyche becomes imbalanced and fails to attain self-actualization.

Self-realization as the actual goal of education, stressed by the Eastern philosophers, is misunderstood by Western educational thinkers who give more importance to the practical application of education. Self-realization as the ultimate aim of education is marginalized from education and viewed as a pursuit of religion. Since religion is based on one's faith, many customs and practices seem to be irrational. One's faith may seem to be illogical in the eyes of others. There also exists a controversy between modern science and religion. Hence, education can sometimes create contradictions in the mind of the believers. A fine example of this contradiction is well explained by Nataraja Guru in his *World Education Manifesto*, referring to the conflict of a schoolmaster who had to make his pupils sing "Rule Britannia" and "Love thy neighbour as thyself" at the same time.

The aims of education are many. Character formation, all round development, self-reliance are some of them. Mahatma Gandhi considers the moral aim or the purity of heart as the ultimate aim of education. Idealists consider the exaltation of human personality as the ultimate aim, while the pragmatists are interested in experimenting with new methods. All these aims are not sufficient to solve the contradictions of the so-called teaching–learning experience.

Nataraja Guru observes the definitions put forward by philosophers as partially valid. According to him, education should treat ends and means unitively and it should be referred in terms of harmony, equilibrium, balance, beauty or proportion in life tendencies (*World Education Manifesto*, 206). Nowadays, teaching–learning process has become a mere passing of information which does not focus on the intellectual or emotional maturity of the child. The current education system to a certain extent fails to actualize the hidden potentials of the child in classroom situations. It focuses on the result of an examination which evaluates the surface knowledge of the pupil. The problem-solving ability or emotional maturity, which makes a person a "good human being", is not considered. Therefore, proper guidance is not given. The purification of emotions or the proper management of a problematic situation is to be given prime importance in education. Guru points out the importance of the dialectical way in education as a solution for this.

Narayana Guru in verse 7 of his *One Hundred Verses of Self-Instruction* describes a way to avoid contradictions and attain Absolute Awareness. Guru says:

To wake never more, ever sleepless to remain, as awareness:
If for this today you are not fit, then in the service
Of those silent ones who ever dwell awake to AUṀ
Absolved from birth, steadily fix your form.

Only a contemplative, who is free from personal interests, instincts and desires, can cultivate wisdom. The common folks are always preoccupied with their own interests and thoughts which are valid to them. As mentioned in verse 4 of *One Hundred Verses of Self-Instruction*, we wake, sleep and satisfy our vital urges and run after food and other needs. In doing so, we always fail to recognize the central awareness in which all other factors can work in unison. But if we adopt a higher level of thinking or a method to solve problems in terms of a greater wisdom teaching, we will realize that our problems are like mirages. Once we enter into the path of real knowledge, our vision will become steady and confusion or contradictions will not bother us.

Here Guru does not want us to avoid any of these needs. But these needs and desires arising one after another may interrupt the actual goal of our life, i.e. attaining unitive vision. To attain such a unitive vision, the aspirant should establish the bipolar relation with a master who is already an Enlightened One. Nataraja Guru says:

If the intervention of the educator in the natural unfolding of the

> personality of the educand is to be successful, it is necessary to establish scientifically correct educational relations between the two persons involved. Here, the understanding of the personal factor and the laws that underlie the bipolar relation are matters of primal importance.
>
> – *World Education Manifesto*, p. 164

To attain wisdom, we should have a clear knowledge about the truth which permeates the subjective self. This is different from understanding ordinary information. It is the unfolding of Self-Knowledge (*ātma-vidyā*). It is the realization that

> I am but a minute particle of God-become-self-unfolded. My existence and God's existence are inseparably one.
>
> – *Garland of Visions*, p. 46

This absolute awareness is hidden from us as a result of *māyā*. Our surroundings, interests, instincts, etc. make us think that what we see around us is true. Only a few aspirants are in search of real wisdom. Some people accidentally come to the path of self-realization if they have some unsolved problems, or a certain type of loneliness which they cannot escape from. But only a real seeker can attain this higher wisdom. Narayana Guru says in *Advaita Dīpikā* verse 11:

> *For a wise man the world is existence;*
> *And subsistence is of value form.*
> *Untruth is not a source of joy; to an*
> *Ignorant man this is not clear.*
> *For one who sees, happiness is a sun*
> *That is real*
> *And for one who cannot see, even the*
> *midday sun is a dark and empty thing.*

In verse 35 of *One Hundred Verses of Self-Instruction* Guru describes the way in which the final wisdom come to the seeker:

Like the dawn all together of ten thousand solar orbs
Wisdom's function comes; Such verily, is that which
Tears asunder this wisdom-hiding, transient māyā-*darkness here,*
And as the primal Sun prevails!

It is nescience which deviates us from real knowledge. It is the root cause of illusions and sufferings. Nescience (*avidyā*) is the inability to discriminate between what is real and what is unreal. As a result, we consider what is experienced through senses as real. In that case, we will not go beyond the experiences through our sense organs. Nowadays, we give more importance to the gratification of our senses. But, we do not know the fact that the same senses may mislead us and put us in danger. To avoid this, one has to develop a conscience which is free from contradictions or rival aspects of life. Nataraja Guru says in his commentary on *One Hundred Verses of Self-Instruction*:

> All that a man actually does in the form of action is the orientation of the spirit or the inner tendencies towards the unitive, instead of the world of pluralistic rival values.
>
> – Commentary by Nataraja Guru, p. 145

Cultural aspects also play an important role in the development of a child. Sometimes it creates an identity crisis which makes an individual timid or violent in terms of his identity. Religion, culture, language, education, social status, etc. may hinder his freedom to think. The I-consciousness of an individual or a community can be clearly revealed when they proudly speak of their own culture or religion and negate the culture and religion of his fellow-beings. We are not aware of the fact that each religion satisfies the spiritual thirst of those who follow them. People always focus on the superficial factors of religion. Narayana Guru in verse 44 of *One Hundred Verses of Self-Instruction* gives a solution for this dilemma:

Not seeing that the various religions in the world
Are essentially the same, advancing various arguments
Like the blind men and the elephant, roam not like fools,
But stop wandering, and calmly settle down.

In the words of Nataraja Guru a person should be able to see the essence of all religions which is distinct from the superficial aspects of religions. These aspects may be different, but all religions advocate the same truth. If we fail to understand this truth, we cannot understand the contemplative values such as universal brotherhood or world citizenship. Guru advocates the method of dialectical wisdom which should be raised to the status of a science and taught in public schools with a definite methodology. If this could be taught scientifically, we can develop a universally tolerant attitude in the mind of the common man and mitigate rivalries. Verse 46 of *One Hundred Verses of Self-Instruction* says:

To vanquish (a religion) by fighting is not possible; no religion
Can be abolished by mutual attack; the opponent of another faith
Not remembering this and persisting in his fight,
His own doom shall be in vain fight for, beware!

A well-cultivated unitive intelligence can break barriers of all sorts. For attaining such a wisdom we have to contemplate on that Absolute Reality. Guru uses the word "Knowledge" for the Absolute and this knowledge shines forth as the universe in the form of five fundamental elements. The same knowledge blossoms as everything and we are a part of it. There is no truth beyond knowledge. Man's difficulty in attaining reality through contemplation is well explained by Narayana Guru in verse 76 of his *One Hundred Verses of Self-Instruction*:

As with a well with measureless sand dropping ceaselessly
Whereon wafting tier on tier fitful gusts prevail,
So too, to the wafting of untruth's hierarchy exposed
Inwardly does the Inner Self multitudinous forms attain

If man is ready to accept his fellow-beings as himself and work for universal brotherhood, all the conflicts in the world can be solved. For that one must identify oneself with the Universal Consciousness and eliminate one's egoistic nature or the I-Consciousness. One should have control over one's senses and continuous contemplation of the Supreme Self will empower us to attain it. Education which focuses on creating such a balanced mind can develop individuals who endowed with higher values and a strong conscience which will not be disturbed when facing the problems of life.

AUṀ

8

A Modern Myth

Sathyabai Sivadas

When God created man, he was endowed with all divine powers. He made use of the power for all his achievements, though he did not know what this power was and how it came handy for him. Ignoring all that, he continued to use it. In course of time, man started to misuse these powers. Instead of doing good, he was precipitating evil. Greed conquered him. He started a search for God to get more power. God got so irritated with the actions of man that He decided to withdraw His power. He cannot take it back to Himself, as it is not ethical to take back something that was given away. So the power has to be hidden somewhere. He called an Assembly of Angels and asked for suggestions.

Suggestions were put forth:

- "Bury it in the depth of the ocean"
- "Hide it on the highest peak"
- "Scatter it among the planets and stars".

God could not accept any of these because all these are accessible to man. He can drill holes in the depth of the ocean, he has already conquered the highest peak and he has ways and means to explore space.

Then a fresh suggestion came, "Let it be hidden in the places of worship, like temples, churches and mosques".

God was vehement in rejecting this, "No, no! They are breaking temples, mosques and churches. They have formed into certain special groups called religions and are bent upon destroying one another's places of worship".

At last God found a solution, "There is only one place on the earth where man will not think of searching for this power. It is the human heart."

So, divine power came to be buried deep in the human heart. Man, in his stupidity, does not realize this.

On the earth, there are some psychopaths called poets and philosophers. They are a troublesome lot. Thousands of years ago, a wise man called Plato realized how dangerous these people are. In his book *The Republic* he wrote:

> Banish poets (and philosophers) from the country. They will give ideas to the people and start revolutions.

These poets and philosophers have a system of communication which is more effective than modern Internet and radio waves. They communicate through heartbeats. The system comes alive in their search for God's power.

A man called Jesus from Nazareth discovered the truth. When he said, "The Kingdom of God is within you", people thought he was insane. When he said again " Love your enemies, because God loves you all", people could not stand the nonsense. They caught him and crucified him.

Another man from Arabia named Mohammad said almost the same

thing. He told the people that there is only one God for all. And he asked the people to distribute 2.5 per cent of their savings to the poor every year (*zakāt*). People did not like it. They wanted to kill him. But he was not mild like Jesus. He took up the sword and fought and maintained himself.

A poet called Rabindranath Tagore from India discovered that God's power was not in the temples or places of worship:

> Your God is not there in the darkest corner of the temple. He is where the tiller tills the land, where the path maker breaks the stones.
>
> – *Gītānjali*

Another poet from America, Walt Whitman by name, searched for God's power in the *Blades of Grass.* Some people understood them, some did not. But they realized there was greatness in what these men said. So they were given Nobel Prizes.

A famous character called Larry, from the novel *Razor's Edge* by another Nobel Prize winner English novelist, Somerset Maugham, came to south India in search of God and peace. He came to know that a thousand years ago, there was a wise man by name Śaṅkara, who had felt God within himself (*aham brahmāsmi*). But Śaṅkara died at the age of 33, and all his teachings remained confined to Sanskrit language which was forbidden to the masses.

But there was a follower of Śaṅkara, by name Narayana, who had experienced the presence of God within him. It was "as if an arid desert was flooded with river water all of a sudden", and "like the light of ten thousand solar orbs rising at the same time".

The poet Tagore came down to meet him and share the experience. The poet was mesmerized by the spiritual radiance of that face. The poet's companion Deenabandhu C.F. Andrews declared, "I saw God in human form. It is no other than Sri Narayana Guru of Malayalam". Mahatma Gandhi also came but he did not find much.

This news spread far and wide in no time. Journalists are a noisy lot. They cluttered and clamoured around Sree Narayana, shooting questions "Are you God? Can you show us God?"

The Guru replied, "*Yes* … Me and God are one … I have become one with God (Ātmāvilāsam – last lines) … I can certainly show you God. … Take a mirror and look, You will find God." They looked and saw themselves. They were shocked and confused. The Guru consecrated a mirror to explain his meaning:

> Know thyself. You are your God. The power to control the entire Universe is lodged within you in mini-scale. Whether you nurture it or destroy it, is totally your decision. If you make use of it not only for yourself, but for others also, it expands and grows. If you use it for yourself alone, it shrinks. If you are true to yourself, it will work. …
>
> The myth continues through twists and turns. …

All Are CENTENARY CELEBRATION OF
WELCOMEPARAM POOJYA NATARAJA GURU
EB.18th 1996.
FERN HILL,

9

Gee You Are You, Too

Scott Teitsworth

In one way of looking at things, "Guru" is the name for the invisible, blissful force which guides us through our lives. One may have a greater or lesser personal relationship with this factor, but despite our varying attitudes about its influence, it is constantly penetrating our life. Those with a theistic or exteriorized orientation tend to associate the Guru with a person, others see it as a benign form of energy, while many others merely take it for granted, carrying on as though they were the only ones "in charge" (triple pun intended). Some, like me, choose D – All of the Above.

The Guru to me is a constant benign impetus that appears throughout our lives in various guises, its existence inferable within whatever tangible events are transpiring. Since most of the so-called tangibles involve interactions with other human beings, the Guru factor is readily associated with those people who have had the greatest influence on us. Mother Nature, for example, may be a tremendous source of inspiration, but she does not deign to explain herself in the ideational terms that form the essential history of our personality. So she should be treated more as a goddess – perhaps even as the manifestation of "the" Goddess – but not as a Guru concerned in some way with an individual person.

I suppose it is a form of prejudice that exclusively associates the Guru with the most beneficial and positive effects, instead of with the entire course of the incarnation. Yet how many of us cripple ourselves spiritually by giving the Divine credit for all the plusses, while taking full responsibility for the negatives upon ourselves? I know I tilt the balance sheet that way all the time, and I am not even a sinner. It must be a deeply ingrained hangover of religious culture disguised as Right Thinking. Yet when I contemplate the meaning of the Guru clearly, the question of credit (and its corollary, guilt) dissolves into nothingness. It is a unitive relation we have, the Guru and I.

Since the immaterial Guru is only perceptible through its effects, it is valuable to examine the most significant moments of our life in terms of the mystical and improbable nature of what took place. Generally speaking, as events occur we have little or no idea of what is really in the works, and only come to realize it later on, after the transformations have taken place. Afterwards we can look back and discern the coherence of what was going on. We should bow inwardly to the way our fate unfolded, often despite our best intentions and expectations.

For my part, it was only after much flailing about on the rock pile of self-delusion, punctuated by a few more or less accidental successes, that I met the Guru as personified in Nataraja Guru and Narayana Guru, through their written works and their ideas as interpreted by Guru Nitya Chaitanya Yati. A couple of heavy dudes, it goes without saying. And they have had an increasingly powerful influence over my thinking throughout my life. Fortunately, they were very open about how we go about manifesting the kind of vision they shared, so I was free to freely flail.

I met then Swami Nitya through the type of "accident" with which spiritual biographies are rife. At least, some magnetic force must have been operating to bring us together out of the chaos of a planet with four billion inhabitants. (Can Earth's population have nearly doubled since then? Oh my God!) I had just severed ties with my family and society, fleeing with my future wife to a remote part of the United States. It was my intention to live simply and practise *yoga* as much as possible, mechanically and surely treading the path to the Divine.

We arrived in the city of Portland from the East just as Swami Nitya was arriving from the West and setting up a class in a local church. We heard of the class by the purest coincidence, yet my wife to be was very insistent on attending. She immediately connected with the Swami, who later shocked both the orthodox and myself by travelling with her for many months as Guru and disciple. Hers was the spiritual magnetism that drew us into the Narayana Gurukula, and while my involvement is more peripheral, both of us felt an instant affinity for Nitya's teaching which has only deepened over the years.

After several evenings in that first American class, on the *Bhagavadgītā* in the fall of 1970, I began to intuitively remember sitting at the feet of other – perhaps even the same – *guru*s in the prenatal past, and began to touch that timeless situation within of a seer surrounded by disciples. I realized that I was in the presence of a true Guru, not just another of the many charlatans coaxing money from the fatuous and gullible. How my heart soared in that presence, certain of a safe and simple passage to the realized state! What a relief to pass all my troubles on to this owlish, bearded foreigner and let him lead me to the Goal of goals!

American ideas of Indian *gurus* mostly came from books in those days and these all speak of the student requesting discipleship from the master, whereupon he performs a few mystical and incomprehensible actions, demands an additional number of unusual services of the student, taps him on the forehead three times and sends him into instant and total realization. So with this scheme and several other preconceptions in mind I entered Nitya's room one day and asked him to be my Guru. He was not interested. He agreed to be my friend, but that was all.

He was not interested!?

Not interested! *That* did not fit the scheme. And with me only two or three steps short of enlightenment and everything so far going by the book! This Swami fellow, the key to all the wonders imaginable, just kicked my whole mental orientation far out to sea where a huge, ugly fish ate it up. To add to the shock, he supplied a few less than complimentary comments about my inner nature, and within a few days I went from being the great and wise disciple to being the biggest fool on the face of the earth. My ego was crushed. My heart felt like a fierce fire, which would be stirred occasionally by piquant observations to allow for more complete combustion. While I imagined Nitya to be the source of this misery, I began to see how in my ignorance I had brought it all upon myself with my baseless projections and that he had properly remained detached and uninterested beyond all my psychic twisting and turning. I, an unprepared neophyte, had merely met the Guru, and from our brief encounter reaped many years of confusion and soul-searching. So much for the mechanical sureness of the path. So much for the certitude of knowing a *guru*. So much for the ease and pleasure of the Way. So many illusions gone. So much humility yet to be cultivated!

Thinking back, most of my early ideas about spirituality now seem so radically unspiritual as to verge on the absurd. I would read or hear about a *guru* and nod my head in sanctimonious agreement with sketchy verbal interpretations of their teaching. But this attitude actually closes us off from the real and potent effect of their Word. In our smug self-satisfaction we desire to be knowledgeable *about* the Absolute as a way of preventing a deeper participation *in* it. We must cast this off in a meaningful way or we are condemned to for ever be the same, rooted in our habitual ignorance.

One day, almost in passing, Nitya said to me:

> You know, Scott, meditation does not necessarily mean sitting in lotus pose with the eyes rolled up. Anything can be a meditation. Playing music properly is a very good way to do it.

Somehow that simple statement took a deep hold on me. A neglected interest in music came back with a rush and a serious study was begun. Guru Nitya has casually reunited me with a part of my *dharma* without my even being aware of it at the time and it has been a major part of my life ever since. In addition to the enjoyment of doing something that is natural to my psychic system, music and *yoga* interact and feed back on one another in mutually beneficial ways. The discipline of studying and concentrating on music has helped me to focus and discard distractions, which has made it easier to pay close attention to the Word of the Guru. And the Guru's teachings help consciousness grow so that it may more easily grasp the complexities of the music being performed. Believe me, every extraneous thought appears instantly as an error during a musical performance!

"Anything can be a meditation." It looks simple in print, but it has repeatedly struck me as an important truth. Especially now, when the traditional yogic approach is becoming a vestige of an ancient world and therefore increasingly inaccessible to everyday folks. Like so many of the teachings of Narayana Guru and his disciples, it breaks through our assumption that *yoga* somehow has a certain structure, can only be done at a certain time (usually "later"), and is confined to those who meet certain criteria or qualifications. We really need to fuse the wisdom and intelligence of *yoga* with our everyday lives, which have become splintered and unrelated to nature and its ways. "Anything" does not really mean anything – it means whatever is appropriate to your particular life and circumstances. *Your dharma*, not the one decreed by some social organization or other extraneous factor, is what is right for you. It does not have to be in music or art or politics. The fundamental realignment that these teachings bring about releases the ability of the individual to be directed to the next project with ever greater balance and dexterity. Even the simplest act can be done more artistically and thus be more satisfying.

Putting people in touch with their true latent abilities seems to be almost the first step that a Guru must make us take. The refreshing nature of being in a Guru's presence comes to some extent from this ability to cut through our individual and collective confusion and expose the core reality, which we in our cumbersome mental dilemmas tend to obscure.

Our worldly life is caught up in pursuing phantom ideas into imaginary situations. When we sit at the feet of the Guru, we can feel this churning mentation calming down, easing off, relaxing, becoming silent. Only then can we hear and absorb what is emanating from him or her. And just as meditation does not always consist of sitting in lotus pose with the eyes rolled up, the Guru is not always hiding within the body of a man or woman. This same process of opening out can take place at a music concert, at a dance performance, or even just sitting by a bubbling stream or a silent mountainside. The principle is always the same: still your mind, let go of your conditioning, be a little humble, and you become free to hear. What you hear is for you alone to know and learn from.

Inwardly I incline before the Guru principle, which has brought me so many blessings through so many wonderful people. And I incline before your *guru*s, who do the same for you, and wear a new face for each and every one. For, I know that these many *guru*s are all one and the same principle, *AUṀ*.

As long as human history continues to be celebrated, Narayana Guru, thanks to those who came after and perpetuated his genius, will be in the top ranks of India's most soul-stirring citizens.

Moments by the River

10

Deborah Buchanan

IN THE centre of the photograph is an upright mirror reflecting the faces of two young women seated in front, looking in. The mirror also reflects the wild meadow around – grasses and flowers, trees at the edge and a blue sky. Unseen but illuminating the landscape is the brilliant sun, itself transparent but allowing the whole world to be seen. This photograph is from 1979 showing a mirror erected near Somanahalli Gurukula in Karnataka, an abstract, neutral "deity" for worship. It is similar to the stone first installed by Narayana Guru in 1895 in a small village of the then Travancore state. In both images, mirror and stone, there is acknowledgement of India's religious history and a sense of sacredness, but the divinity is presented without social inflections. The mirror and the stone image by their abstractness include all of the worlds we inhabit – the objective transactional, the personal subjective, the dreamy interlude, each of which arise from the unspoken depth of the Absolute.

This photograph and Narayana Guru's revolutionary gesture at that first temple dedication are emblematic for me of the Narayana Gurukula's presentation of Vedānta: nothing is excluded or rejected but, as Nataraja Guru so very aptly taught, all is related within the framework of horizontal and vertical coordinates. How we understand ourselves and our world are the essential factors of a spiritual life. We do not reject the world but let go of our sense of possession and agency. At the intersection of the horizontal and vertical coordinates is the neutral centre, a glowing, eternal, locationless point. None of the *guru*s of the Gurukula has taught a structured practice. Instead insights and immersions are presented that can lead to a transparency of vision, an experience where we recognize an absolute unity already and always around us.

My first acquaintance with Nataraja Guru was at the World Parliament of Religions in Shastamcotta, Kerala, in 1971. When I arrived with Guru Nitya and Jean-Pierre Rothart Devos, Nataraja Guru walked up to us, offered his hand to shake and introduced himself. He was quiet, solemn, not at all resembling the fierce *guru* of rumours. The next morning he sat on a bed discoursing on *Ātmopadeśa Śatakam* to a room of students. Behind him the sky lightened with dawn and he spoke in English peppered with Malayalam, Sanskrit and French. This unself conscious philosophical pondering, the continued sharing of his inquiries, the unassuming personal dignity – all of these are characteristic of my short time with him, where it is also necessary to mention his sharp, Puck-ish humour. Over the following years his translations of Narayana Guru's works and his erudite commentaries on them and on the *Bhagavadgītā* allowed me to more fully appreciate the Gurukula teachings.

For me these teachings centre around the 100 verses of *Ātmopadeśa Śatakam*. In verse 1 the word *karu* is used to describe the Absolute Reality – also described as the primeval cause or the Universal Self. It is what moulds us and what gives meaning and truth to our lives. It is the word or experience where immanence and transcendence come together. It is from this experience of the *karu* that our questions arise and it is where our answers resolve. Slowly and with care throughout the entire set of verses, Narayana Guru explicates varying aspects of the Self. What is the foundation of our daily life? Who are others and how do we relate to them, and what are the ethics of doing so? What are fear and death? Is there evil? What is ignorance? All of this is explored in depth and then presented with a limpid simplicity. Reading these verses and the commentaries by both Nataraja Guru (intellectual and revolutionary) and Guru Nitya (psychological and contemplative) and Guru Prasad (open and generous) allows one to study varying approaches. In all of them, the core is a philosophy which is grounded in intellectual clarity, limitless sympathy, and responsibility and deep reverence.

When Narayana Guru travelled throughout south India he was aware of the cruelty that underlay much of the social world. He did not, however, coalesce groups to fight these problems. Wherever he went he inspired listeners with his spiritual visions and supported steps in concert with them. When confronted by oppression, he opened his arms, so to speak, to include those very opponents. It was a quiet and slow process, one which began to profoundly transform his world. The "other" is only you – there is not another. When we see darkness is not a separate, evil intent but an ignorance that can be enlightened, we too are opening our arms to the other. We have, as Guru Nitya wrote, an unlimited liability to each other. The choice presented by the Gurukula is not between engaged action and indifference, it is between an encompassing world view and a bifurcated one. The Absolute is unequivocally shown as a holistic comprehension that supports our lives, not merely a philosophical term.

Over the last five decades I have been involved in the Narayana Gurukula and its teachings. Visits and classes at the *gurukula*s in India, travels throughout the world with Guru Nitya. Hosting the weekly study groups here in Portland and participating in online classes. Editing the English language *gurukulam* for ten years. Reading and writing and inner pondering. A family life, work involvement. All of which provide ample occasions to practise wisdom in action!

On the occasion of the *Śatābhiṣekam,* the *1000 Full Moons years anniversary of Guru Muni Narayana Prasad,* I silently bow my head in respect to the *guru*s of the Narayana Gurkula and its continuing lineage of teachings.

It has been noted that one cannot step into the same river twice, as neither the river nor the person remain the same. Yet one can sit quietly for a few moments and watch the water flow. It gurgles and burbles, speaking an enticing language. There is also a silence underneath that language, as well as mystery, both of which call to us. We can see below the ripples a glinting thread that continues on throughout the changing water. We sit and listen, grateful for the abundant generosity and grace of the world. Grateful for all the teachings. Grateful for the Nothing and the Everything.

11

Sacred Art and Sacred Seeing*

Andy Larkin

RELIGIOUS art, the use of visual images in contemplative life and practice, has a long and complex history across the entire spectrum of world cultures. Equally complex and varied are the attempts at written explanation of these diverse phenomena. Some religious arts are iconic in nature and personifications of deities given plastic form are highly developed in both Eastern and Western art traditions. Other traditions, including Judaism, early Christianity, Islam and early Buddhism have preferred aniconic representations of religious ideas; Islamic art in particular used geometric patterns as metaphors representing metaphysical processes and structures. However, all of these kinds of visual expression stand as superficial in relation to the deeper reality they are designed to reveal, because, to put it bluntly: the Absolute cannot be represented.

---

* At the outset, the present writer wishes to express his profound gratitude to Guru Muni Narayana Prasad, whose lifetime of sacrifice has preserved the pure vision of Vedānta upheld by all the *gurus* of the Narayana Guru Paramparā. To him this essay is respectfully dedicated.

What, then, are we to make of any claim that any art is in any sense "sacred"? The world's spiritual masters and philosophers have given the notion of sacred art, at best, a mixed reception. Plato was well known for his suspicion of artists of all stripes. Others, such as Thomas Aquinas, held that art's sacredness lies in its process aspect, and that "art is the imitation of Nature in creative action", a view affirmed by the twentieth-century art critic and proponent of Oriental aesthetic ideas, Ananda Coomaraswamy. However, to consider the role of visual art in contemplative practice more closely, one must consider a more fundamental question: what is the general status of sense experience itself in a contemplative context?

A consideration of the work and example of Narayana Guru may offer some insight. The well-known first two verses of the Guru's *Ātmopadeśa Śatakam* read as follows:

> *Permeating the knowledge which brilliantly shines*
> *at once within and without the knower*
> *is the* karu; *to that, with the five senses withheld,*
> *prostrate again and again with devotion and chant.*
>
> *The inner organ, the senses, the body,*
> *the many worlds known by direct perception – everything,*
> *when contemplated,*
> *is the glorious embodiment of the sun that shines in the sky beyond;*
> *this should be known through relentless search.*

These verses, taken together, refer to the entire unitary field of consciousness, as well as the phenomenal realm of discreet senses and their objects, which are its "glorious embodiment". The first verse lays out a vision of the unitary field, with its passing veiled reference to the chanting of *OṀ*, while the second proposes that, without exception, all the elements of our experience find their being in the *karu*, which is their divine origin. The Guru here evidently advises the spiritual aspirant to restrain, rather than destroy, sense activity. So what is the nature of this restraint and what is the nature of relentless search?

In his enumeration of inner faculties in verse 2, the Guru analyses the components of phenomenal experience using terms belonging to Sāṁkhya and Yoga: the inner instrument, senses and sense objects. In similar terms, Patañjali's *Yogasūtra,* at points, offers a detailed analysis of the psychology of sense restraint, and in one interesting passage (Samādhi-Pāda 17-18) refers to a mode of prolonging perceptual confrontation to prepare for *savitarka samādhi*, a preliminary "seeded" form of *samādhi*. Such states are occasionally experienced by many, for example, when they are overwhelmed by the beauty of a sunset. Patañjali's comments provide clues as to how such a *samādhi* state might be cultivated or prolonged. The commentary of Guru Nitya Chaitanya Yati is worth quoting at length:

> As a self-discipline, the *yogī* can take any ... experience (of perceptual confrontation) and prolong the duration of the modification of the inner organs in an identical state by precipitating a reverberation of the same order continually and contiguously so that consciousness is held in the same location for an extended time. When that is attained, one is not a mere enjoyer (*bhogī*) but becomes a disciplined perceiver who is oblivious of time. In such a state one is a *yogī* who is experiencing concentration, *ekāgra*. This is when the neophyte *yogī* is using a positive experience as a plank for Yogic discipline and consequent achievement of contemplative balance.
>
> In the same manner the *yogī* can use the negative counterpart, the cessation of an experience, for another discipline. Where a cognition

disappears into a state of oblivion, the entire stream of consciousness can also vanish. Perception (is) … transcended and the *yogī* remains in a state of absorption. For such absorption … absorption into the vanishing point of a perceptual encounter (can be a lead). – Yati 2009: 83

Returning to *Ātmopadeśa Śatakam,* Guru Narayana offers another interesting insight into the question of sense restraint in verse 8:

Enjoying the five fruits, such as beauty,
mounted on a foul-smelling gun and evasively flying back and forth
are five birds; having brought them down, through an inversion,
that radiant inner awareness should fill one's entire being.

Here the Guru uses a conceptual ideogram composed of several metaphoric elements. In the first, a *yogī* sits beneath a tree, laden with appealing fruit (sense objects) that attracts hungry birds (senses). In the second, a shotgun blasts a spray of pellets to bring them down. The verse highlights the importance of an "act of inversion", the cancelling out of a perceiving subject and a perceived object, precisely defined in the Patañjali *sūtra* quoted above. The "act of inversion" represents a "turning within". It is not so much a destruction or denial of sense experience, as an acknowledgement of the radiant origin that unites the perceiver and the perceived. The *fig.* 11.1 combines the two metaphoric elements of the verse into a single graphic form.

Let us now return to our original question about whether any art can merit the designation "sacred", and attempt to

fig. 11.1: Ātmopadośa Śatakam verse 8

apply the observations outlined above to the appreciation of a religious work of art from the European tradition, "Magdelene with the Smoky Candle" by the Baroque era French artist, George de la Tour (1593–1652) (*fig*. 11.2). The picture, painted by an artist with a profound ability to portray fugitive human emotion, shows the one-time prostitute and disciple of Jesus, Mary Magdalene, alone in a darkened chamber cradling a human skull in her lap and meditating before a candle, the sole source of illumination in the room. This theme is the subject of hundreds of paintings from the medieval era onward; here however it is treated with a truly sublime sensitivity. Mary Magdalene sees the candle, but what holds her attention is something else, something that the artist cannot show and something that the viewer can only infer. Her gaze is steady. The conventional iconography tells us that she is pondering the transitory nature of life, but the non-engagement of her gaze with the external world shows us something else perhaps. And that is the prolonged non-dual identification of the repentant Mary, a woman of great but transitory beauty, with the burning down of the candle and the cancellation of both into spiritual understanding.

fig. 11.2: Magdelene with the Smoky Candle

Admittedly, such an interpretation of this painting lies within the realm of projected speculation. But it raises a final and perhaps crucial issue. Here, the present author must recount his own personal experience viewing this artwork, some years ago, at the Los Angeles County Museum of Art, in the presence of several friends. The friends moved on, but I remained captivated by the image. After some minutes, I became aware that my relation to the painting was the same as that of the young woman to the candle. I had been stunned into a prolonged, deepening silence of identification with the object before me.

It may well be that some dimensions of the question we have briefly considered here can only be approached in purely subjective terms, and for this no apologies need be offered. For it remains the case that a work of "sacred" art is never a phenomenon existing in and of itself, having satisfied certain formal requirements: a "sacred" artwork requires "sacred seeing".

Reference

Yati, Guru Nitya Chaitanya, 2009, *Living the Science of Harmonious Union,* New Delhi: D.K. Printworld.

12 How My Guru Revealed Himself to Me

Sathyabai Sivadas

WHEN Swami Tyagisvaran wrote to me that "a valuable article to be included in the volume about Guru Muni Narayan Prasad is expected" from me, I felt flattered. It is a rare privilege and I thank all those who joined together to confer this honour on me. Guru Muni Narayana Prasad is important to me in a very special way, though we do not know much about each other. Guru Muni happens to be one of the persons who guided me in the correct path, in my discovery and realization of Narayana Guru as the ultimate in *guruhood.*

I must start the story from an earlier background. The first revelations of the Guru were during my childhood days spent with my grandparents at the seaside village of Kayikkara, about 5 km south of Sivagiri. My grandfather, Sub-Registrar Velayudhan was an ardent follower of Narayana Guru. Visit to Sivagiri on Sundays and holidays was our regular routine. While our grandparents sat in meditation under the jackfruit tree in front of *Guru-samādhi* (the old thatched shed), my brothers and I would run around playing. Very often grandfather would make us sit beside him and tell us stories about the Guru. We would listen with wide open eyes, but I should confess that we did not understand half of what he said. We were too young to understand. But we had a feeling, "Here was a great man, respected by grandfather, we should also respect and obey him because grandfather says so." At home, we were made to learn *Daivadaśakam* and *Ārāyukil Andhatvam* (poem by Kumaran Asan) by heart and recite these during prayers. We did not know who composed them. But memories remained ingrained.

Time rolled on. On completing higher education, I got a job as Lecturer in the Educational Service of Andhra Pradesh state, the newly-formed state of Telugu-speaking people, after the States' Reorganization in 1956. My first posting was at the Government College for Women, Guntur. My father took me to Guntur to join duty. As I interacted with my colleagues, I began to notice a world totally different from the one in which I was brought up. In this context the Guru's *viśvarūpam* slowly began to unfurl before me.

The first instant was an enigmatic question. My colleagues discovered that I was from a fairly affluent family, my father was a well-placed government official, who could educate his children and maintain his family without loans, he could easily give me lots of gold, pay a good dowry and get me a good husband. Then why did he send me away to this far-off place to work and earn? Why did I choose to come away leaving all the comforts of home? I did not know how to explain to them that I simply wanted to work. I was educated and wanted to make use of it to earn my livelihood and incidentally, for the benefit of others also. Hidden somewhere in the folds of my brain was the principle that a person, whether man or woman, who remains idle and lives on the produce of others is exploiting the society; they are a menace to the society. Are these not the words of Gurudeva that came to me through my grandfather? I knew, but I did not know how to explain it to others.

The second occasion was my marriage. I was twenty-two years old, the age to fall in love. I met the young man, who was destined to be my husband and fell in love. He was a native of Andhra, employed in the Railways. His brother contacted my father with the formal marriage proposal. My father came to Vijayawada to meet the young man, spent a day with him to study him. My father was satisfied, he went home and told mother, "The young man is alright, from an ordinary family, is educated, has knowledge, has a good job, behaves well, he does not smoke or drink. Moreover these two are in love. We will get them married." At that time I did not know the full significance of these words, but it was revealed to me later, while I was translating *Śrī Nārāyaṇa Dharmam* and *Jāti Nirṇaya*; my father was following Gurudeva's words *ad verbatim* while settling my marriage. Those words were the polestar of guidance for my parents. Caste, religion or region was not at all an issue. My life was moulded by Guru's words. (We were married at Sree Nārāyaṇa Mandiram, of Mambalam, Madras, on 12 May 1960 and it lasted for more than sixty years of wedded bliss until Divine Will called him back.)

The next revelation was more drastic, acute and disturbing. Soon after marriage we started to look for a house for rent at Guntur where I had the first experience of "caste". We found houses in decent localities with the notice, "To let". In most of the houses one half is occupied by the house owner and the other half is given for rent. When we approached, the first question we faced was "Are you brāhmaṇas?" When we say we are not, the response would be that the house was already given. This went on repeating. I wondered what caste has to do with paying rent. I once asked, "Then why don't you remove the 'To Let' board?" Without giving any answer, they stared at me and closed the door. I did not understand. My husband explained the situation. In those parts brāhmaṇas give their houses for rent only to brāhmaṇas. They do not want a non-brāhmaṇa to live near them or occupy their house. It will defile their spiritual purity. They cannot share their well-water with a non-brāhmaṇa. Even tap-water, the non-brāhmaṇa had to wait till the brāhmaṇa had collected all the water he needs. Moreover, if a brāhmaṇa happens to see a non-brahmaṇa for the first time in the morning when he gets up, it is a sacrilege. He has to undergo ritual purification. While a brāhmaṇa is taking food, if a śūdra happens to see that, the food is defiled, it has to be thrown away, and the brāhmaṇa has to starve for the entire day! And so on *ottallaho jāti komaraṅgal.*

I was petrified. To me, who was brought up saturated with the unitive philosophy of "One Caste, One Religion and One God for man", all these sounded absurd and substandard. I could not conceive how even educated people could be so narrow in their thinking and behaviour. My husband explained the intricacies of the caste system and its practice and how the hierarchies are strictly maintained in the society outside Kerala. I started to observe the people around me. I saw that their souls were crippled with the cancer of caste. Among the students there were caste groups. In the hostels, there were caste groups. Among my colleagues, who are all doctorates and postgraduates, there were caste groups. When I told them that I don't understand the meaning of this caste, they thought that I was an idiot. For a moment I felt lost and helpless in this ocean of caste. But I realized: there is a *nāvikan* to save me from this *bhavābdhi* and I am already in the life boat. It was certainly the implicit faith and rational acceptance of Gurudeva's principles that prompted my parents to reject all fallacies and let me join Andhra Government Service and settle my marriage, which was "inter-caste, inter-state and inter-linguistic". Quite a revolutionary step sixty-two years ago! And was it not Divine will that brought me to a family who does not care a damn for caste among these caste maniacs?

I started to think. Why do my people, people of Kerala in general, think and feel differently from the people of Andhra in these matters? The figure of Narayana Guru emerged with renewed brilliance. It was he and his teachings that were responsible for this difference. I have read that he had effectively organized a "bloodless revolution" in Kerala. Now I understood what a revolution is. It is not protest march and slogan shouting; it is a fundamental transformation in the mindset, thought process, attitude and ethics of the people in general. He has enabled the people to develop a new value system based on human equality, integrating the spiritual and the temporal. This superhuman task the Guru has achieved within a short span of forty years. With this revelation, the stature of my Guru rose higher and higher in my mind, my casual respect for him was replaced with awe and admiration, bordering on devotion.

My interaction with the student community of Andhra Pradesh revealed another great truth to me. I had been working in government colleges where nearly 20 per cent of the students were of SC&ST communities, from rural background, who were admitted on "reservation" (in the 1960s). All of them were given a monthly allowance in the name of scholarships. Unfortunately these "Ambedkarites" did not take education seriously. Most of them would come to the college for scholarship money. They would come and ask me for attendance and permission to be away from the class, so that they can go out and do something to earn their daily bread. Gurudeva's words flashed through my mind "Poverty and ignorance are the basic reasons for all social evils". These poor students need their attendance to get the scholarship and to take the final exam. Just before the exam, they would mug up some questions and answers from "guides" and scrape through the exam to get their degree and again a job on reservation. They said they could "some how manage" (They start working with no knowledge in their brains! No wonder why people support anti-reservation.) They are simply reducing the entire process of higher education to a mere farce by this distorted thinking.

I was totally upset with this intellectual emptiness, self-degrading attitude and misplaced objectives. Poverty and ignorance have combined, fertilizing each other creating this devastating by-product. I felt the contrast in the attitude and approach to education between the students of Kerala and the students of Andhra, especially among the lower castes. I could clearly see it was Gurudeva's endeavours that led to this intellectual renaissance. As early as 1905 itself, Gurudeva had started an evening school at Sivagiri for the poor agricultural labourers' children, who had to work in the landlord's farm during daytime. He had seen that poverty should not stand in the way of education. Those poor children could work to satisfy their master and earn their wages and pursue their lessons. The practice continued until Gurudeva abolished child labour among his followers, much earlier than our governments thought of it. The child's Right to Education became a rule in India only in 2012, Gurudeva had acknowledged the issue and found a solution a hundred years earlier. Gurudeva's practical wisdom in preparing people to accept changes, emerged with resplendence in my mind. There were evening colleges in Andhra in those days, but these were meant for people with white-collared jobs, not for the farm labourers!

Another point flashed in my mind, Gurudeva's instructions to the volunteer speakers of SNDP (1905) was, "Tell the people about the importance of education". I was sure my students in Andhra were not told about the importance of education – real education, acquiring the power by which your personality is modified and polished, not the process by which you become a pseudo-scholar with a trail of degrees. They should know how real education can liberate them from spiritual, intellectual and social enslavement. They should know that "Knowledge is Power"!

I decided that I must introduce Narayana Guru to these people and tell them how he had liberated the downtrodden masses of Kerala through education and spirituality. So, during Ambedkar Centenary Celebrations, I presented a Paper on Sree Narayana Guru at a National Seminar organized by UGC (University Grants Commission) at Siddipeṭ. It had the required effect. The intellectuals and Ambedkarites picked up the idea. Osmania University introduced Sree Narayana Movement as a topic for study in the postgraduate syllabus of Sociology and Political Science. I published my paper as a booklet *SNG: The Practical Philosopher*. Demand came from the Telugu-speaking public to know more about this "wonderful Guru". My husband and I jointly wrote the second book, *Sree Narayana Guru: The Social Philosopher of Kerala.*

This is the book which brought me to Guru Muni Narayana Prasad. I requested Swamiji to kindly go through the book and give his opinion. He opened my eyes to certain realities. As a true *guru* who is concerned about the disciple's welfare, he gently pointed out the mistake in my perspective, that I was missing the spirituality of the Guru. I was only beating around the bush, I did not study or understand the Guru properly. I was only trying to explain what the Guru did and how he did it, not why he did it. I did not explain clearly why a *saṁnyāsī* like him – a person who has renounced every worldly ambition – came back to the midst of humanity to share their joys and sorrows, to alleviate their suffering, to elevate their standard of thinking and lifestyles.

Guru Muni Narayana Prasad talked to me for more than an hour and I listened very carefully. I imbibed every word of what he said. He explained clearly why Nanu Asan withdrew to a forest to meditate. Like the Buddha, he was troubled in his conscience. The pathetic conditions of people around him disturbed his peace of mind. He found most of the traditions meaningless and absolutely wrong. He wanted to find out what is right and wrong, what is the Truth, why there is so much suffering in this life, what is the meaning of this life and what is his role in it. During all his wanderings, he found only problems, not answers to the problems. He had to find answers within himself. Our sages have discerned the secrets of the Universe through meditation and mystic visions. Nanu Asan also followed their steps. For long hours he "remained in contemplation harnessing internal energy and wisdom". What he experienced through withdrawal and meditation for six long years was an exultation of his self into the Eternal Existence or the Universal Consciousness. As he is a part of the Universe, the reverse became true for him that the Universe is part of him. This great awakening bestowed upon the young Guru an all-inclusive Vision of Unity. Everything in this universe is a part of a Whole. All are one. The difference between "you, he and I" disappears.

To a person who has identified himself with the Universal Consciousness, any custom or tradition that denies this "One-ness" is utterly baseless and a negation of Universal Consciousness. Once he had discovered the Truth, it became his responsibility to take this wisdom to the people who are struggling in ignorance. The seeker of Truth became a seer of wisdom and assumed the role of the Guru. A *guru* is one who can transform the riddles of life into experiences of bliss.

As a teacher of wisdom, he saw humanity around him struggling in the high seas of life without a polestar of value to guide. Religion, which should have been the guiding force, was reduced to a bundle of traditions, customs and superstitions and raised an impenetrable iron curtain between man and his God. Narayana Guru felt it was his *svadharma* to revalue and restate religion and all that religion connoted, to suit the idiom and climate of the time and make it acceptable to the people. He had to cleanse the religion of all unhealthy traditions He started with temples, which he converted into vehicles of transformation.

The second task he had to do was to enlarge the scope of vision of the people he led, beyond their own personal self and immediate circle, into a wider horizon encompassing all around them and humanity at large. Only then can human beings be liberated from the clutches of narrow sectarianism which bound them down to self-centred closed circles. He must usher in an era of harmony and reconciliation. People must be made willing to accept the equality of the fellow human being, as spiritual brothers (*ātmā-sahodarāra*).

Therefore, when casteism, religious bigotry and superstitions in the name of religious traditions were rampant, the Guru came out to the people with his Unitive Philosophy of One Caste, One Religion and One

God for Man. From the level of intellectual dialectics, Advaita was brought to the status of a way of life by him. And in this process a number of titles were conferred on the Guru: a social reformer, a religious reformer, a spiritual preceptor, a redeemer of the people, a saint, a *yogī*, a humanist, The Father of Renaissance of Kerala and so on.

I congratulate Narayana Gurukulam for being the first and foremost institution to liberate Narayana Guru from regional limitations and project him as *viśvaguru* (A Universal Guru)! And I am proud to be given a humble role to play in this great endeavour.

I hope I have explained my indebtedness to Guru Muni Narayana Prasad. Every time I come to Sivagiri, I visit and talk to him. If there is any doubt lurking in my subconscious mind, it will be cleared after a few minutes talk. I always remember that he is the one who showed me the correct path – *nerām vazhi.* I pray for his welfare and hope he would enlighten many more like me.

13

Close Encounters with the Fourth Dimension

Swami Vyasa Prasad

I FIRST met Guru Nitya in 1979. Not long after discovering the wisdom of the *Bhagavadgītā* and the writings of Swami Vivekananda.Words of wisdom gave a new meaning to life. I was left with no choice but to abandon the world of work in search of this newly-discovered dimension. I had become a seeker. Sensing my predicament, my father told me about a *gurukula* not very far away. I found the serene place, barely 2 km from my home. Those were turbulent times, both inwardly and outwardly. Around that time I had also got admission to a private university in Chicago, USA and was to apply for a student visa soon. Meeting Guru Nitya and his group of disciples was like entering a magical circle. The morning classes on the *Tao Te Ching* were paradoxical to my ears but strangely comforting to my heart. My first friend Peter Oppenheimer was carefully noting down the readings and responses, later published as *Meditations on the Way*. I felt like Hamlet, ambivalent about the possibility of studying in an American university and the reality of being in the presence of a Wonder Guru. I could not make up my mind and decided to let the *Tao* take its course. I presented myself to the Visa Officer in Chennai somewhat half heartedly, only to be rejected on grounds that I could not prove my non-immigrant status. This is how I came to be in the company of Guru Nitya and a group of his Western disciples who subsequently became my best friends.

From that moment onwards Guru Nitya became the most important influence in my life, shaping my thoughts, capturing my love, affection and service, gracing me with the happiest moments of my life. At the same time I was getting the correction that I needed. I could endlessly listen to his calm yet authoritative voice, marvel at the depth and meaning of his words, and let my mind be filled with adoring wonder. A little parental pressure made me attempt another job between 1980 and 1983 this time in Darjeeling, a beautiful hill station in the Himalayas. But by then I was already smitten by the Guru. I read his commentary on the *Bhagavadgītā* every day before and after work. The proprietor was pleased, but I knew that my heart lay in the distant south, far away from the Himalayas. After a year I had a few weeks of annual leave and I promptly joined Guru Nitya, becoming part of his entourage travelling through Kerala. It was an unforgettable experience meeting beautiful people and having sublime experiences. I cannot forget the first time I heard the *Saundarya Laharī* being chanted, and Narayana Guru's *Cidambara Aṣṭakam* sung by a group of musicians. It was awe-inspiring. I knew that I need not go back to the job, but a sense of obligation and an inability to make a spontaneous decision made me return for another year so that I could officially resign and present myself before Guru Nitya at the Fernhill Gurukula. His first question was, "Can you type?" I could. He promptly proceeded to dictate a short article for a college magazine: "A Parable for the Educated". This was my first assignment. In subsequent years I became a veritable "Gaṇeśa", a dedicated scribe, taking down dictations, word processing them and passing them on for editing. Thus study and work combined in a very rewarding manner.

Not long after, I hatched a scheme to get Guru Nitya and my family to meet each other. My father was the headmaster of a renowned school. I told him that Guru Nitya was a very good speaker and so could he be invited to give a talk to students? Father agreed. Then I asked my mother if she would host a lunch for the Guru and a few disciples. She agreed. On the chosen day, Guru came home and had lunch and then gave a talk to the students. Later we all sat in the headmaster's office for a cup of coffee. Guru was talking about his forthcoming trip to Singapore. I still had a hangover from my job days and so I asked him whether I could get a job in Singapore. Guru's answer was most unexpected. He said, "If you like to travel with me, get your ticket and join me". Thus I spent two weeks with Guru at the Singapore Gurukula, followed by two weeks at the residence of one of his admirers, followed by ten days in Malaysia. On my return to India, I became a regular member of his travel entourage to Delhi, Sikkim and various other places around Kerala. In 1990, while at the home of N.C. Kumaran in Chennai, Guru again surprised me by giving me the name Vyasa Prasad.

One day Guru handed me a box containing the most exquisitely typed manuscript of *The Psychology of Darśanamālā*, which had been prepared by Scott Teitsworth. He asked me to find a good printer and suggested a few names like Vasanta Press, at the Theological Society in Chennai, and the Aurobindo Press in Pondicherry. When I reached the Ooty bus stand an overnight bus for Pondicherry was ready for departure. I promptly boarded it and was at the Aurobindo Press the next morning. But they were too busy and suggested that I should try the All India Press. There I met Saphal, the manager, who agreed to print the book and thus started my relationship with manuscripts and galley proofs. Subsequently Nataraja Guru's *Autobiography of an Absolutist* was printed and later *The Life and Teachings of Narayana Guru*. These projects introduced me to the writings of Nataraja Guru. I was immediately drawn to his writing, both in content and style, which vaguely echoed my own science-based public school education. Though I could understand only very little, a long association with the writings of Nataraja Guru had begun.

Sometime in 1991 Guru Nitya asked me if I would like to go to Fiji. The present Guru, Muni Narayana Prasad was at that time heading the Gita Ashram in Ba and was to return to India. I immediately agreed. It took about a year for the work permit and airplane ticket to arrive. Guru then asked for a set of his *kavi* clothes to be brought and handed them to me. This was on 24 January 1992. The subsequent years as Swami of the Gita Ashram in Fiji were the most productive and progressive periods of my life. I made three trips to India from Fiji and during the last one in 1998, I asked Guru whether I could be with him. He said I need not go back to Fiji, but again a sense of obligation made me return. I was never to meet Guru Nitya again.

The fascinating encounter with guruhood continues today by the grace of Guru Muni Narayana Prasad. His unfailing support, gentle kindness, love and his penetrating wisdom opened up new understanding, especially of Narayana Guru's works. The *Śatābhiṣekam* is an auspicious occasion to express my gratitude. Before coming to the Gurukula in 1979 at the age of 26, I had not heard the name of Narayana Guru. As a child

I visited the Ramakrishna Mission in Fernhill, but could not find any meaning in the picture of a simple man in a *dhotī* seated cross-legged. All through my college days I considered myself an agnostic. Today I feel I am sitting on the shores of an ocean of Narayana Guru's teachings; gradually the rising tide engulfs me and I let go off everything that I was grasping, absorbed deeper and deeper in the wisdom of Narayana Guru's words.

AUṀ TAT SAT

366

14

Narayana Guru's Prasādam

Deepanjali

NARAYANA Guru guides our lives through his life and teachings. Narayana Gurukula represents Guru's vision of Truth. Our lives are abundantly blessed by the Gurukula's *guru–śiṣya* lineage who unfailingly upholds non-dual wisdom. Gurukula's present Head, Guru Muni Narayana Prasad is indeed like Narayana Guru's *prasādam* (blessings) for all of us. Having lived a life of ultimate dedication to Narayana Guru, Guru Muni shines brightly like the sun itself, dispelling the darkness of ignorance and misery from our lives.

Guru Muni's wisdom teachings are amply made evident through the many commentaries that he has written on Narayana Guru's works and the Upaniṣads. Guru has extraordinary prowess to express complex philosophical ideas and arguments in simple terms. In all his commentaries, Guru takes great care to explain the context in which any given idea is developed. He foresees the main questions that can potentially arise in the reader's mind and most effectively addresses them. In a number of his works, Guru Muni has used the Socratic method of making the listener raise questions pertinent to the concept under discussion, thus making sure learning is an active process. This method has been hugely popular with numerous learners. Further, just like Nataraja Guru and Guru Nitya, Guru Muni seamlessly switches between traditional Vedāntic wisdom and modern scientific principles in his works. He brings out the unitive field of Reality where philosophy and science meet on a common ground.

An analogy that Guru Muni recurrently uses in his commentaries to explain the oneness of *sat* (unmanifest existential aspect of Ultimate Truth) and *bhāva* (manifest form of Ultimate Truth) is that of gold and ornaments made of gold. This analogy is arguably the most suitable one to pinpoint the unity of *sat* and *bhāva*. Gold can take numerous forms like different ornaments or the form of ore itself. However, the gold content which pervades the forms is one and the same and it is indestructible. Guru Muni has made use of this analogy to explain this basic tenet of Advaita many times in his classes also. Each time Guru Muni explains the analogy patiently and points towards its hidden meaning so that learners achieve clarity of understanding.

One of the core philosophical questions which Guru Muni diligently highlights in many of his writings is about *karma* or action. Who is the real doer of *karma*? By elucidating and elaborating on the teachings of Narayana Guru and other previous Upaniṣadic *ṛsi*s regarding this central question, Guru Muni states that *prakṛti* or nature which is the functional mode of Reality is the true doer of actions and not we individual human beings. And, moreover, *prakṛti* does not take any ownership of these actions. Hence, these *karma*s are nothing but functional modulations of

Ultimate Reality. A *jñānī* or a realized one does not think that he/she is the doer of any *karma*s.

Yet another aspect that Guru Muni deals with in his works is the phenomenon of miraculous events or doings that seem to be part of many wisdom teachers' lives. Many people tend to give undue importance to the so-called miracles that happened in the lives of Jesus Christ or Narayana Guru. Guru Muni reminds us that we cannot completely explain even the mundane things that we are familiar with in our everyday life. For example, when we sow the seed of a particular plant, although we are used to seeing the sapling sprouting out of the seed in a few days' time, we do not know exactly how these changes are happening. It is only the familiarity that makes us feel that sprouting of the sapling is "natural". We have no idea about all the potentials hidden in this universe to make claims that some event is "unnatural" or "unexplained". Guru Muni points out that life itself is a mystery which plays out in the Ultimate Reality.

Another aspect about life which Guru Muni draws our attention to repeatedly is the *ānanda* content of Reality which binds all of us together as One. The life on this earth for human beings, animals and even non-living beings is designed in such a way that one ensures the happiness of the other. It is our failure to note this *ānanda* aspect of subsistence that makes us do selfish deeds and cause misery to others. A realized one sees only one reality abiding as the *ānanda* in everything and everyone. Hence, the most effective way of augmenting mutual love and harmony among human beings is to make each one realize that all are part of one Reality.

The ideas discussed above are regarding just a few aspects of the multifaceted manifestations of the one reality that Guru Muni deals with in some of his works. Numerous are such concepts in philosophy and life which Guru has conclusively explained standing firm on the unitive ground of non-dual wisdom. However, in his commentaries Guru also reminds us that Truth is not revealed through intellectual deliberations, but through a process of contemplative meditation (*tapas*). Thus, truth is to be realized in oneself and as oneself. Rightly, the one who realizes the truth lives inseparable from it. Truth will be revealed in all his thoughts, words and actions as exemplified by a few day-to-day instances in Guru's life as I have known them.

Once Muni Guru slipped and fell and broke his leg. One of Guru's *gṛhastha* (householder) disciple came to know about this and felt very sad about Guru's mishap. Over a telephonic conversation with the Guru, the disciple lamented, "Oh, my Guru!! It is so sad that you broke your leg. And I am worried whether someone will be there at the *gurukula* to attend to your needs while you lie bed-ridden?" In reply, Muni Guru simply said, "What if someone is there to take care of me? What if someone is not there to take care of me?" These casual words which Guru uttered are nothing short of a lesson in equanimity, a virtue so natural to a *sthitaprajña*. Going beyond the dualities of comfort and discomfort, pain and pleasure, the *sthitaprajña* remains undeterred in his life.

Going beyond pain and pleasure does not mean becoming passive or indifferent. In fact, a *yogī* exercises his mind, intellect and body in a way which ensures the upkeep of the world including himself. Once a small epidemic of eye infection was rapidly spreading among *gurukula* inmates in Varkala. Muni Guru briefly moved away from Varkala to avoid getting infected. Thus, while a *yogī* is always cognizant of the transcendental truth in every situation, the transactional validity of the situation in real life is never lost upon him. A *jñānī* sees that one and the same truth forms the essence of a piece of stone and a piece of gold. However, this does not mean that he uses gold to serve the purpose of the stone or vice versa. For a seeker, there is much to learn from carefully observing the life of a seer until the seeker himself or herself obtains the eternal clarity of vision of truth.

Once I was passing through a tough phase in my life. Some experiences made me judge both myself and others in an unkind way. I made a phone call to Guru who patiently listened to all my woes. He passed no judgement on the situation but offered some deeply insightful ways to look at events and cut down exaggerations. At one point I described myself as "diffident and emotionally hypersensitive person". At this, there was silence at his end. I began to sense that the description which I gave myself is just spurious. It was an invalid description. The truth abiding in me is amenable to no description, whether good or bad. And that is the same for everyone else too. Definitely, a *guru*'s silence is as eloquent as his words, if not more.

Guru's blessings do not come from outside. Rather, it wells up in one's own heart, cutting away the dreary dross of dead thoughts and habits. It is both easy and difficult to follow his path of light. Easy because one need to be just oneself in this path. Difficult because at each step in this path an "i" should yield itself to be effaced by the I. Where does the path lead to? Guru says that "the culmination of realizing the effulgence of consciousness is becoming consciousness itself".

15

Basic Lessons on India's Wisdom

Pooja Lal

The *Basic Lessons on India's Wisdom* is written by Swami Muni Narayana Prasad of Narayana Gurukala, Varkala, Kerala. He wrote this book to educate the younger generations of Indians who live in other countries, such as the US, about the basics of Indian's wisdom heritage. It answers most of the questions the younger generations are likely to ask regarding religion and culture. It helps to incorporate the essence of India's wisdom in the reader's life.

This book personally resonated with me because it answers a lot of educational questions I had regarding my Indian and Hindu roots. Here are some of the lessons I learned:

- The Upaniṣads stand first in Hindu scriptures.
- There are two *itihāsa*s and they are the *Rāmāyaṇa* and the *Mahābhārata*.
- The Upaniṣads stand for wisdom. Which means a proper understanding about ourselves, this world and the unseen reality.
- In the Hindu religion, the Upaniṣads belong to the *jñāna-kāṇḍa* and

the Vedas belong to the *karma-kāṇḍa.*

- What is the "I" in all of us?
- When we see something, it is not really the thing that we see, but only the qualities that the thing possesses. What really exists as a thing-in-itself is always invisible.
- Heaven, Hell, Vaikuṇṭha and Kailāsa are all in our mind.
- No one in the world can have ownership over anything because everything including us belongs to a total system. Our life becomes happy and peaceful when we find ourselves a part of the integrated, eternal flow of life.
- We should not try to avoid necessary actions, but at the same time we should not do anything as our personal *karma*.
- Ignorance of the Reality is called *avidyā* in Vedānta which is a state of darkness. Those who live in such a state are called *asura*s.
- Accumulating wealth is a very painful affair. After it is accumulated it is more painful to keep it safe. So wealth is pretty much a big jar of suffering.
- Wealth is needed in life but we should not live for wealth. In India, Lakṣmī is not considered a Goddess worthy of worship.
- Knowing oneself is called *ātma-jñāna*. You will know God when you know yourself.
- If anything becomes lovable, it is only because of man's urge for self-happiness.
- When someone touches the feet of a *guru* or *swāmī* he/she is showing his/her willingness to follow the *guru* or *swāmī*'s footsteps.

The wealth of knowledge and information stored in this small book is immense. I think every young Indian should read *Basic Lessons on India's Wisdom* and educate themselves about Hinduism and Indian culture. There is also a Malayalam version of this book available called *Arivinte Aadhyapadangal*. This is a book written for the English-speaking younger generation and is organized in a question and answer format to portray the Upaniṣadic method. I would like to thank Swami Muni Narayana Prasad for writing this book and giving me a newfound perspective on Hinduism and Indian culture.

പുരസ്കാരസമർപ്പണം
KAIRALI
KAIRALI
KAIRALI

16

Philosophical Traditions of India and the Empowerment of Youth from the Viewpoint of Swami Vivekananda

C.M. Neelakandhan

SWAMI Vivekananda's inspiring words and dedicated efforts for the cultural synthesis, social reformations, and the upliftment of the poor, the downtrodden and the oppressed yielded far-reaching results in Indian life and its culture. The effects of Swami's sincere efforts are strikingly evident even today and shall, quite affirmatively, continue to bear fruit in the coming centuries as well.

Throughout the course of a lifetime of boundless preachings, Vivekananda's profound vision centred mainly on the youth. He believed that it is the budding ones who should be strengthened and nourished with the cultural reformations that are to be effected in the country; he wholeheartedly envisaged well-formulated reformations that empowered the youth. Vivekananda placed his trust sincerely upon the tenets of Indian philosophical traditions, interpreting them thoroughly for the remoulding and reshaping of his dear country in all respects. In this regard his sanguine vision was realistic, deeply humane, free of all biased pre-notions, practical and one that imparted strength of all kinds to the mind and the intellect alike.

Religion and Spirituality in Vivekananda's Views

Subjected to reformations on such grounds, Swami Vivekananda, thus, revised in various ways Indian traditions of knowledge, spirituality and religion. Along with these, he was ready to welcome and incorporate Western thoughts which are equally relevant and useful. In order for the everlasting blossoming of a new Indian society rooted in self-confidence, humanism, moral and spiritual strength, and equality for all, Swami Vivekananda contemplated on the effective moulding of a honest synthesis of the two above-mentioned worlds of philosophical thought.

For many centuries Vedas and Upaniṣads, and later philosophical traditions of India have had their deep-rooted seats in religion and spirituality and have been moulding and influencing the life of Indian people. But in the course of time a slow and gradual deviation from their true spirit, vision and purpose seemed apparent. Of course, this is an unavoidable destiny that every religion or social or political movement is bound to degenerate and deviate from the basic concepts, values and visions in the course of time. And this declining movement was highly noticeable in the time of Swami Vivekananda, which must have prompted his motivated actions.

Great social, religious or political leaders take up the task of reformation according to the needs of time. Vivekananda, respecting the inevitable urgency of his time, took up this important task of reformation, in regard to the religious, spiritual and philosophical traditions of India. He has given various definitions for religion in different contexts, shedding light to his novel ideas on the purpose and utility of religion and spirituality in both collective and personal life:

- "Religion is the manifestation of divinity already in man."

  – *CWSV* IV: 358
- "Religion is the realization of God." – *CWSV* I: 417
- "Religion is the realization, not talk, nor doctrine, nor theories, however beautiful they may be. It is being and becoming, not hearing or acknowledging. It is the whole soul becoming changed into what it believes."

  – *CWSV* VII: 396

In all the above-cited and other similar statements, Swami Vivekananda poignantly stresses on the true spirit of religion and philosophy, all properly reflected in the Vedāntic, Upaniṣadic and later systems of philosophical traditions. This holds true not only with Vedic religions, but is found in other religions of Indian origin, like Buddhism and Jainism, and also in religions of worldly order, in the likes of Islam and Christianity. After all, the basic texts of all religions stress universal values of common and everlasting interests, viz. that of humanism, love and compassion to all, ethical values, development of the individual and personality in total, and the like. Naturally, one may be tempted to ask, "so, then, where does the contamination occur?" The deviation from the main and true path of all religions happens when their teachings are interpreted and practised with biased motifs.

Jñāna-kāṇḍa and Karma-kāṇḍa

From very ancient days, different schools of philosophical thoughts prevalent in India have sustained their own interpreted versions of the Vedic tradition. Among them, the *jñāna-kāṇḍa* and the *karma-kāṇḍa* schools of philosophy are the most important. While the Brāhmaṇa texts, which describe the *śrauta* rituals like *yāga*s, give stress on *karma-kāṇḍa*, the Upaniṣads preach *jñāna-kāṇḍa*. Though attempts have been made by great scholars like Śrī Śaṅkara to interpret texts like the *Bhagavadgītā* – the monumental Indian scripture representing the synthesis of *karma* and *jñāna*, the two latter-mentioned currents of thoughts have always moved in divergent paths in our tradition. Śrī Śaṅkara, in his *bhāṣya*s on the Upaniṣads, the *Brahmasūtra* and the *Bhagavadgītā*, had established *jñāna-kāṇḍa* over *karma-kāṇḍa*. It is a generally accepted notion that in Indian philosophic tradition, *karma-kāṇḍa* has only secondary importance, the highest of eternal universal ideals being represented in the *jñāna-kāṇḍa*. Swami Vivekananda accepts this aspect of our philosophic tradition as useful and important.

Smṛti texts, the later developments of the ritualistic aspects of *karma-kāṇḍa* tradition, clearly prescribes social customs based on religion, ritualism or belief. However, Vivekananda rejects these trends because, as it is very evident, such rituals or *ācāra*s will easily give way to *anācāra*s or *durācāra*s. This is why they have to be approached and accepted with a reasonable mind, to be discarded if found disadvantageous for the further development of a healthy society. But, on the other hand, the true values of *jñāna-kāṇḍa*, representing humanism, feeling of brotherhood and sisterhood, experience of moral and ethical values like *dayā*, *kāruṇya* and universal oneness are always needed and are useful to an ideal society. What Vivekananda means by statements like "manifestation of divinity already in man" and "religion is the realization of God" is the experience of the high values of *jñāna-kāṇḍa* tradition already mentioned. This true and utilitarian aspect of our philosophical tradition is stressed again, of course following the flawless path of Swami Vivekananda, by later thinkers like Swami Ranganathananda, in his monumental works like *Eternal Values for a Changing Society*. "Eternal values" here denote the values of *jñāna-kāṇḍa* tradition noted above – values that are never-changing, always applicable and a need for an ideal society at all times. Values of changeful nature are those pertaining to the ritual tradition or *ācāra-kāṇḍa* or *karma-kāṇḍa,* which are liable to change or adapt in accordance with the place we live, the food we take, the environment in which we dwell and other such socio-cum-cultural or historical conditions. Whatever be such circumstances, one find himself perched in, one must always stick to the universal values of the *jñāna-kāṇḍa*, that which always found deep admiration in the hands of Vivekananda.

God in One's Own Self, in the Form of Power

Swami Vivekananda carves out divinity and realization of God as the ultimate developments of an individual on the path of the Universal Self, where one triumphantly realizes one's own unlimited power and energy. The narrow or weak impulses of egoism and selfishness usually rule over men. One should therefore rise from such ungracious levels to that of unselfishness, before realizing the impersonal and universal truth in him. This is what Vivekananda underlines as the true purpose of spiritual pursuit based on philosophy. His life vision was to impart this spiritual understanding into the young minds, for he maintained that it is only through such pure understanding that one may develop universal feelings of humanism, compassion, adherence to truth, ethics, etc. At the same time, with such an understanding, they realize the eternal and unlimited power inherent in them, whose limitless potency could inspire hard work and dedication for the upliftment of the society.

Thus, terms like God, *Brahman* and Ultimate Reality found in different philosophical systems, according to Vivekananda, are the representations of the unlimited or internal power that is inherent in all. Due to personal limitations, like egoism, attachment to worldly things, passions and the like, man, in the usual course, does not realize or thoroughly understand it. One can get rid of the former impulses through different courses prescribed in various philosophical systems of India, leading to the realization of the unlimited inherent power. Thus, Vivekananda's view of religion, God or philosophy is the realization of the true Universal Soul or power in oneself. This idea that God is the internal power of and in all is not a notion "beyond" the individual, has been hinted by the Upaniṣads and other canonical texts, both indirectly and otherwise. This idea finds explicit remarks in Vivekananda and that is why his doctrine can be called a kind of neo-Vedānta.

For Swami Vivekananda, this kind of feeling or experience should not be mere dogmas or theories embedded in religious texts alone, but rather should be an experience by which each individual transforms himself to the impersonal level and works with dedication and commitment for the upliftment of the society as a whole. The youthful age is the best period of one's life when one can most enthusiastically work for the society. That is why Vivekananda persistently advocated youth empowerment as a means of the benefit of the society. Thus, for Vivekananda, religion and spirituality are pragmatic tools for cultural reformation. In this respect,

Swami Vivekananda, as in many other aspects of our tradition with similar coherence, adheres to the teachings of Buddhism that preached a pragmatic philosophy for the upliftment of the common folk, the down-trodden, the oppressed, the poor, unsupported, unprotected and the suffering. One of Vivekananda's primary agenda was to boost these sections of society which comprise the major components and always need care, soothing, protection and upliftment.

Thus, Vivekananda, as is discernible by now, accepts and reasserts the good and the practical aspects of our religion and philosophy, vigorously synthesizing them with the values of life, finally resulting in the building up of a new Indian society endowed with confidence, courage, and moral and spiritual strength. Vivekananda encourages the youth to adopt such values. In a different context, this statement of Swami Vivekananda about religion and spirituality, like other similar statements, further reaffirms this vision:

> Each soul is potentially divine. The goal is to manifest divinity in man that can be achieved by controlling nature, external and internal. Do this by either work or worship or psychic control or philosophy, or one or more of all these and be free. This is the whole of religion. Doctrines or dogmas or rituals or temples or forms are but secondary details. – *CWSV* I: 257

The Lost Cub Brought up by the Goat Community

While commenting on his vision on Indian spirituality, Swami Vivekananda gives an apt example for the above-mentioned interpretations:

> Once a lion cub happened to get lost in the jungle, separated from its parents in the midst of the intense wild. Incidentally, a herd of goats living in the forest found the lost baby and took good care of it from

> thereon, bringing him up as one among their own. Along with the herd-family, the little king began to wander in the forest, eating grass and wild leaves, just like the herd of goats. In time the baby grew, developing bodily features resembling that of a lion's, like clotted hair (*saṭā*), protruding long teeth and sharp big nails on feet. Nevertheless, the "lion-ness" in him went unaware.
>
> Around that time a fierce lion appeared in the nearby forest, causing the goats to leave their community settlements and run away in severe fright. The now all grown-up cub too tried escape, engulfed in fear. The sight of a young and healthy member of the wild royal descendence running away shamefully confused the invading lion. Days passed by and one fine day the wonderstruck lion visited the forest once again. This time, calm and composed, managed to discreetly isolate the goat-brought-up lion from the mild group. On a secluded portion of the greenish wild, the matured lion advised the younger one, telling him that he is not one among the goats to run away in fear, but rather one of "superior" order, a lion – the king of the forest, who is blessedly endowed with all strength and confidence to kill and eat all other animals of the forest. Yet the domesticated lion stood unconvinced of the fact of his existence.
>
> Then the elderly lion took him to the banks of a river and they compared each other's reflections. The first one told the latter that both of them display similar clotted hair and also resemble each other in their long protruded teeth and sharp big claws. At last the newly-arrived lion, glancing at its own image in the water, roared loudly and asked the little one to repeat similar roars. It did so, quite correspondingly, inducing fright, and, at that very moment, the younger realized that "I am a lion with all might and power in me".

Quite similar is the way how Vivekananda illustrates his vision too. There is a lion-like power and might or similar strength sleeping in all. But none do realize this fact due to many varying reasons.

Our efforts should primarily be to know and realize the unlimited power and confidence that we have already in us, the result being the growth of the individual from specific limitations to that of the attainment of a state of universality. By this, each individual gets access to all that is ordinarily inaccessible – to plan and execute high ideals and visions for the upliftment of the society, to work with universal vision, high ethics, morality, adherence to the truth and confidence for the happiness and well-being of the whole universe. Thus, divinity or God is within each individual itself, its realization and experience enabling in one the strength to work for the society with an impersonal outlook. Young generations can do this more effectively, and so, Vivekananda, always advocates the empowerment of the minds of the young inclining in such a manner. For this, he accepts the true spirit of our philosophical traditions and advocates its practical implementation, for its beneficiary advantage in our personal lives and that of the society.

Courage, Alertness, Activism and Freedom from Fear

For the empowerment of the youth, Vivekananda unreservedly accepts from the great Upaniṣadic tradition, traits like courage, alertness, freedom from fear and continuous activism. He quotes the Upaniṣadic statements like *abhayam vai brahma* (fearlessness is *Brahman*), *uttiṣṭhata, jāgrata, prāpya varān nibodhata* (Arise, awake, approaching the best of Masters, do get enlightened) and interprets them according to his vision for the empowerment of the youth and dedicated work in regard to the upliftment of the society. *Brahman* (Highest Reality) of the Upaniṣads is actually the state of fearlessness. One who is free from all kinds of fears only can develop his personality and work with a dedicated mind for the society. Fear is the cause for all kinds of restrains. Once rid of fears of all kinds, one's mind will become free of all biased and ego-centred actions. That freedom of mind will give one the courage to indulge in hard and dedicated austerities for the development of one's own personality and that of the society. One should always be alert in mind and active throughout for the attainment of such state. This final attainment must be the goal of each and everyone in the world, transforming the whole of society to a higher level. The concept of renunciation (*saṁnyāsa*), the observance of austerities (*vrata, niyama*, etc.), the study of sacred texts from the *gurus*, *dhyāna*, *tapas*, etc. prescribed in the Upaniṣads will help one in attaining this goal. Thus, Vivekananda interprets the tenets of the Upaniṣads in accordance with his vision, which is often called "practical Vedānta" or "Neo-Vedānta".

Śaṅkara's Intellect and Buddha's Heart

Swami Vivekananda accepts ideals like ethics, morality, compassion towards the poor and the oppressed, charity, sharing the sufferings of those tormented with poverty, disease, dishonour and such from philosophical systems like that of Buddhism and Jainism. Since Buddhism and Jainism contain antagonistic views against the Vedic tradition in many respects, they are considered as *nāstika* philosophies. But the humanistic ideals of such systems of philosophy mentioned here celebrate worldwide acceptance and general recognition, the final result being that of Buddhism and Jainism gaining status as international religions of India, spreading their philosophic ideals all over the world. Vivekananda does not hesitate to accept the ideals of Buddhism and Jainism having the fervour of love and compassion towards the struggling and the poor and at the same time synthesizing them with the Upaniṣadic views, all for the empowerment of the youth and for laying the foundation stones for an ideal society. It is only with the development of this compassion and love towards the poor and the oppressed that one may work in the society for its upliftment. It is in this respect Swami Vivekananda assumes a unique and vibrant place among the social reformers of India. Truly, Vivekananda is a rare spiritual leader with a "Buddhist heart and a Śaṅkara intellect rolled into one being" (Ramakrishnan 1980: 64-65).

Vivekananda and Rāja-yoga

Swami Vivekananda always highlight the principles of Yoga philosophy, one of the six systems of Indian philosophy, for developing the personality of each individual to the realm of universality, as we have already discussed in the preceding headings. Vivekananda preaches, through the principles of Yoga philosophy, the attainment of discipline and control over the body and mind by practising various methods like *yama*, *niyama*, *āsana*, *prāṇāyāma*, *pratyāhāra*, *dhāraṇā*, *dhyāna* and *samādhi*, the *aṣṭāṅga*s of Yoga, as described in the respective philosophical system. He accepts these principles and advocates their practice for the empowerment of the youth, maintaining relevance and importance throughout all times in relation to the development of an individual to work with dedication and commitment for the upliftment of the society.

In 1907, for the very first time, a dedicated file of Vivekananda's complete works (in English) was collected and published from Advaita Asrama, Almora, in eight volumes. Later, various editions have appeared from different Ramakrishna Asramas and other publication firms, adding further volumes to the earlier editions. In 1979, the eight volumes of the earlier editions were translated and published in Malayalam from the Sri Ramakrishna Asrama, Puranattukara, Trissur. The Malayalam translation has been brought out in seven volumes, carefully rearranging the matter of the English edition according to the respective topics dealt with. Vivekananda's concepts regarding the *yogatraya* (*bhakti-yoga*, *karma-yoga* and *jñāna-yoga*) are found in the first volume of the Malayalam edition. The second *khaṇḍa* of the first volume is devoted to *rāja-yoga*, the most important method of Yoga. It is given in eight *adhyāya*s. These eight *adhyāya*s mostly contain his views on *rāja-yoga*, based on the speeches he delivered in New York and other places. The text of the *Yogasūtra* of Patañjali, containing Malayalam commentaries and notes, has also been included in the first volume of the Malayalam translation.

Rāja-yoga: The Most Important among the Yoga Systems

From the different references found in various ancient texts, it could be concluded that, in India, different systems of Yoga philosophy were in vogue. In the *Bhagavadgītā* there is a reference to a Yoga system that had lost its continuity due to the long lapse of time:

> *śrībhagavān uvāca*
>
> *imaṁ vivasvate yogaṁ proktavān aham avyayam* ।
> *vivasvān manave prāha manur ikṣvākave 'bravīt* ।।1।।
>
> *evaṁ paramparā-prāptam imaṁ rājarṣayo viduḥ* ।
> *sa kāleneha mahatā yogo naṣṭaḥ parantapa* ।।2।।
>
> – *Gītā* IV.1-2
>
> This Yoga system was advocated by God Kṛṣṇa to the Sun-God who, in turn, taught it to Manu. Manu passed it on to Ikṣvāku. Now, in the course of time, it is lost or untraceable.

The treatment of the Yoga philosophy in the *Gītā* starts with this statement.

In the *Yogatattvopaniṣad* too there is a reference to the many systems of Yoga that prevailed in India:

yoga hi bahudhā brahman bhidyate vyavahārataḥ ।
mantrayogo layaścaiva haṭho 'sau rājayogataḥ ॥ (– I.19)

According to this reference, four systems of Yoga prevailed in India, viz. *mantra-yoga, laya-yoga, haṭha-yoga* and *rāja-yoga*. *Mantra-yoga* is a system followed by Śaivas and Śāktas. *Haṭha-yoga* is a system concentrating on the discipline of the body, practising of which would train the body in different ways for achieving superhuman powers. It is said that by practising *mantra-yoga* and *haṭha-yoga* one could release the weight of the body and freely rise up to the atmosphere or impart overweight to the body for resistance. The basic texts of these Yoga systems are not popular now. It is known that the Śaivas and Śāktas preserve some of the texts related to these Yoga systems and practices. They preserve them as secrets, unwilling for public disclosure. *Laya-yoga* is a system that is known to have developed in connection with the Vedānta philosophy. The method of the unification of the self with the universal *ātmā* is the subject matter of *laya-yoga*, which too has lost its theoretical or intellectual popularity now. The basic texts of *laya-yoga* too have gone out of demand.

Yogasūtra of Patañjali

Rāja-yoga, having gained much popularity and relevance in modern times, is clearly described in the text *Yogasūtra* of Patañjali, which is included in the six systems of Indian philosophy, viz. Sāṁkhya, Yoga, Nyāya, Vaiśeṣika, Pūrva-Mīmāṁsā and Vedānta. Each of these systems, except for the Yoga system, has different respective schools and divisions, developed under various teachers over time. There are other philosophical texts as well that contain the principles of Yoga, mainly *rāja-yoga* like the *Bhagavadgītā* (in which there is a major section dedicated to the Yoga discipline), *Tejobindūpaniṣad, Yogatattvopaniṣad, Chāndogyopaniṣad, Sāṁkhyakārikā, Muṇḍakopaniṣad, Śvetāśvataropaniṣad, Yogaśikhopaniṣad* and *Mahopaniṣad*. Swami Vivekananda accepted the *Yogasūtra* of Patañjali for the formulation of his views on *rāja-yoga*, at the same time taking relevant tenets related to Yoga from all other sources as well, from the varying texts that gained mention above.

Aṣṭāṅga

The main aspects of *rāja-yoga* are the eight paths that are to be dedicatedly observed. They are: *yama, niyama, āsana, prāṇāyāma, pratyāhāra, dhāraṇā, dhyāna* and *samādhi.*

> *yama-niyama-āsana-prāṇāyāma-pratyāhāra-dhāraṇā-dhyāna-samādhayaḥ aṣṭau-aṅgāni* ।   – *Yogasūtra* II.29

Yama is defined as the observance of austerities, like *ahiṁsā* (non-violence), *satya* (adherence to truth), *asteya* (non-stealing), *brahmacarya* (life of celibacy) and *aparigraha* (restrain from the longing for the possessions of others).

Niyama denotes cultivating holy and virtuous ideals in mind, like *śauca* (purity), *santosa* (happiness), *tapas* (penance), *svādhyāya* (studying holy scripts) and *Īśvarapraṇidhāna* (dedication to the feeling of God).

The succeeding stage, *āsana* (postures), helps one attain control over his or her body. To develop high ideals and thoughts in mind, one has to train the body so as to have control over it. Practising different postures aids this. The *Tejobindūpaniṣad* says that one can follow any posture by which the feeling of the unification with *Brahman* (Universal Soul) is achievable. The postures one practises for the purpose should afford feelings of easiness and joy in him:

> *sukhenaiva bhavet yasmin ajasram brahmacintanam*
> *āsanam tadvijānīyāt anyat sukhavināśakam* || – I.25

Such practice yields a pure and clean body and mind, free from all negative impulses and ready to accept of high and noble ideals and create superhuman powers.

PRĀṆĀYĀMA

Practice of *prāṇāyāma* is the fourth stage of *rāja-yoga. Prāṇāyāma* has a great role to play in concentrating and centring the powers of the mind to a meeting point and strengthening it. In the usual course a person is unaware of the hidden or latent powers of the body or mind that one actually possesses. The reason being that we have no devices to know them in the common life. One has to dive deep into the mind and realize or recognize it. The whole energy that is in one's mind and body should be under control for that. This is what is meant by *prāṇa* (energy) in *yoga*. The most visible part of it is breath. Through controlling one's breathing process and practising other methods of *prāṇāyāma*, one could slowly get control over the mind and the body. In due course one gets to realize the unlimited power that he or she potentially holds, the realizing of which gives strength and confidence to work freely for greater causes and for the upliftment of the society. Vivekananda recommends such a systematic method for the empowerment of the youth.

Vivekananda explains the course by further dividing the *prāṇa* into two: *ādhibhautika* and *ādhyātmika*. The *prāṇa* that pervades the whole universe is *ādhibhautika*. All kinds of energy or power that one could see in the various objects of the universe, say the sun, moon, fire, wind and stars are all included in *ādhibhautika*. By practising *prāṇāyāma*, one can train the mind in such a way that all powers of the universe could be brought under the control of the mind. Thus, everything in the world comes under the decisive spell of such a person. He will have immeasurable command over the celestial and other objects of the universe; he will have unbelievable control over his own mind and senses and this unique power could be rightly envisaged for the good of the whole universe. We rightly call such personalities having achieved such rare heights as *yogī*s or *siddha*s. The unification of the *ādhibhautika* and *ādhyātmika prāṇa*s could be achieved by *prāṇāyāma*, resulting in the acquisition of unlimited internal power in order that one may carry out justifiable actions without fear or hesitation for high and noble causes. Vivekananda urges the youth to methodically attain such a pleasant stage which, if strived for sincerely with hard work and dedication, is not beyond the reach of any. Those (the youth) getting empowered in such a way, Vivekananda stresses, are capable of rebuilding and developing the country in new and distinct ways.

PRATYĀHĀRA, DHĀRAṆĀ, DHYĀNA AND SAMĀDHI

The heading adequately suffices for the next four stages in the practice of Yoga: *Pratyāhāra* is the withdrawal of the senses inwards, for only then shall one become the master of his own senses. In a regular scenario man is the slave of his senses and the senses are his masters, commanding and instructing in accordance to their whims. But by practising *pratyāhāra* one reverses the usual order, gaining mastery over his directive senses. The result is that one may enjoy total freedom, stripped of any kinds of attachments.

Pratyāhāra slowly leads to *dhāraṇā*, which is the attainment of the power to fix the mind in some points, withdrawing it from others. This will help one to concentrate the mind on any matter of personal inclination or wish, thereby granting more focus for advocating it with much precision.

As we proceed further, *pratyāhāra* and *dhāraṇā* pave the way to *dhyāna* (meditative mood), which is the next in line. If the mind is fixed on a particular point, all the acquired power through the relentless practice of *yoga*, gets concentrated on a fixed point, blissfully flowing and getting concentrated. This adorable stage is the experiencing of endless power or energy and delight.

Coming to the final stage, *samādhi*, the experiencing of the state of super-consciousness, we happily distinguish it as the realization of unlimited power or supra-consciousness or divinity or *Brahman* or the God in oneself. Such an experience is the birthright of each and every individual. But due to many phenomenal reasons and limitations of various kinds, men are not able to fully recognize or realize or experience it.

Swami Vivekananda desires all, especially the youth, to strive hard for its realization, and thereby bring beneficial and hard-earned fruits of sincerity and dedication for the society.

Yoga and Tenets of Philosophy Practised by Vivekananda

Not only did Vivekananda advocate and champion the various Yoga principles and the tenets of Indian philosophical systems – both *āstika* and *nāstika* – making them relevant and useful for nurturing a new society, but made them a practical certainty by realizing them in his own life. Thus, his life itself became his philosophy. We are accustomed having high regards for great philosophers and social workers like Mahatma Gandhi or Sree Narayana Guru. The various incidents and episodes in the life of Vivekananda and his preachings clearly demonstrate how he put into practice the salient features of the philosophical systems that India has been preserving from her very ancient days. Such incidents and episodes of his life have been recorded in various works, such as his many lectures on various topics. Many studies and researches on Vivekananda's life portray such motivating phases of his fruitful life.

Following are some such selected instances, enabling us to know how he made such ideal principles a practical reality by translating it into his own life:

1. From a very young age, Vivekananda was a serious and devoted practitioner of *dhyāna*. Once when deeply indulged in *dhyāna*, in the quiet company of his dear friends, a frightening cobra happened to pass by the meditative group. Perceiving approaching danger his friends ran away in fear. But Vivekananda, untouched by the changeful world of happenings, continued his penance, totally absorbed and unaware of the outside phenomenal movements. Slowly the cobra slithered away, without causing hurt or pain. This inspiring scene portrays the unfluttering state of mind Vivekananda attained in *samādhi*.

2. Vivekananda was always courageous and fearless, the two important traits that the Indian philosophical systems like Vedānta advocate for practice. Upaniṣadic statements like "do not fear" (*abhiḥ*) or "the Ultimate Reality is fearlessness" (*abhayam vai brahma*) establishes this. Throughout his life Vivekananda practised fearlessness and courage. Coupled with the power of reasoning, these traits made his

mind powerful enough to argue against the prevailing superstitions, wrong beliefs and the *anācāra*s and *durācāra*s that prevailed. Vivekananda rejected all these with courage and reasoning power, accepting only those that are useful and relevant at all times, for the development of the individual as well as for the welfare of the society as a whole.

3. Many recorded incidents of his biography note courage and fearlessness. In his younger days he used to cheerfully play with his friends by hanging on the branches of the neighbour's tree. In order to drive away the children from such youthful acts, the house owner told the little ones a make-believe story of the tree being possessed by a ghost who will strangle their gentle necks, thereby ending their lives. All the children believing this, stood numb in panic and fear, except Vivekananda, whose courage outwitted such baseless utterances.

4. In yet another interesting incident from his sweet days, Vivekananda and his close friends leisured in a lovely boat travel. Unfortunately, one among them felt uneasiness and vomited in the boat. Reaching the destination, the boatmen rudely compelled the young lot to clean and tidy up the boat. His friends became frightened hearing the sharp words of the boatmen. But Vivekananda, requesting help from a nearby group of British armymen, single-handedly managed the situation, conversing with the foreign officials in broken English.

5. An apt example of Vivekananda's fearlessness and courage is his famous act of swimming across the ocean at Kanyakumari till the faraway rock, his brave destination, an admirable and adventurous act signifying the *samādhi* of his mind, his power of determination,

untiring enthusiasm, readiness for undertaking hard and dedicated life-missions and risk of any kind and the like. On that day of his great dive into the deep oceans, the coastal surroundings was lonely, not even a wandering soul was there to hear the distant cry for help (if any!). The ocean was vast and the rocky destination was afar. Possibilities of adverse danger were many, looming silently in the wavy waters, in the likeness of being hit badly by underwater rocks or being swallowed by big hungry creatures residing underwater or even the simple idea of being carried away into the deep waters by the tremendous waves. However, not taking into consideration such dangerous calamities and confusions, Vivekananda marvellously crossed the ocean and reached the rock-end, courageously floating past all the looming threatening possibilities and risks.

With this act Vivekananda was in fact preparing his mind, or strengthening it, for all the upcoming life challenges, risks and hardships, all awaiting mutely as the time comes when Vivekananda fearlessly embarks on the visionary journey of moulding a steady and developed India.

6. Once Vivekananda, while staying with the ruler of the Province of Khetri, for three days straight went without sleep and food, constantly answering the questions and queries of the many admirers who arrived from different parts for eager gazes and adoration. This is the quality of a true *yogin*, to practise work with all vigour, even if it means going empty stomach or devoid of rest for days.

7. Once visiting England, Vivekananda took a casual walk with his English friend and the latter's wife. A wild ox ran into them for an

unanticipated and sudden attack. The couple started running with all efforts and might, the lady even falling down on the ground, trembling. But Vivekananda, with his celebrated courageousness, stood before the ox with folded hands. The thought of the charging ox ending his life ran through his mind. He even calculated, in the midst of all the chaos, the exact point on the ground where he will fall down, if hit by the wild animal's accelerating aggression. But the native animal, instinctively recognizing the courage of his foreign rival or prey, returned slowly, before exchanging exasperated glances at Vivekananda for some time.

8. Another similarly chilling episode was once recorded when Vivekananda was amply strolling through the wild. He was very hungry and thirsty and tired after his long walk through the isolated woods. At that time a mighty lion, out of nowhere, appeared in front of him. Projecting neither fear nor confusion, Swamiji stood gazing at the powerful animal, focusing steadily on its royal eyes. For hours they stood in motionless tension, exchanging diverse glances, with the animal king now and then throwing frustrated and clueless roars. Finally, the ruler of the wild returned for reasons only accessible or available to his defeated mind.

9. Vivekananda consistently conducted his social and effortfully conceptualized mission for the poor, on those who were suffering from poverty, ignorance and infectious diseases. This vision he imbibed from the philosophies of Buddhism and Jainism.

10. One among the preachings of Vivekananda, a soft one, was to habitually play football everyday, thereby strengthening the body and its health. For he absolutely believed that only a strong and

healthy body could flower great wonders. He even advised that the teachings of *Bhagavadgītā* could be better grasped and understood by strengthening the body (thereby corresponding health too) through regular active sports like football.

References

Bhagavadgītā

Lakshmikutty, N., 2012, *Swami Vivekananda on Indian Reconstruction*, translation into Malayalam by M.S. Nair, Vadakara: Malabar Institute for Research and Development.

Pāścātyaparyaṭanam, Vivekanandaswamikal, Puranattukara: Sri Ramakrishna Ashramam, 1966.

Principal Upaniṣads with Śāṅkarabhāṣya, Delhi: Motilal Banarsidass, 1978.

Ramakrishnan, R., 1980, *Swami Vivekananda: Awakener of Modern India*, Madras: Sree Ramakrishna Math.

Tapasyananda, Swami, 1988, *Swami Vivekananda: His Life and Legacy*, Madras: Sree Ramakrishna Math.

The Complete Works of Swami Vivekananda (*CWSV*), Almora: Advita Ashramam, 1968.

Vivekānandasāhityasaṁgraham, 3rd edn, Puranattukara: Sri Ramakrishna Ashramam, 2007.

Vivekānandasāhityasarvasvam, Malayalam translation, Puranattukara, Trissur: Sri Ramakrishna Ashramam, vol. I, 1979.

KAIRALI
KAIRALI
KAIRALI

17

An Advaitic Christology and Liberative Spirituality for Integral Renaissance of India

Acharyasri

Introduction

ALONG with the Mataji and a *sādhaka* from Dharma Bharathi Ashram I had paid a visit to Swami Muni Narayana Prasad at Narayana Gurukulam, Varkala, a year before the outbreak of the COVID-19 pandemic. This meeting with him was arranged by Shri Sebastian Thenassery, a disciple of Swamiji and a student of Advaita Vedānta. As a parting gift Swamiji had given me a copy of his book, *Christ The Guru* which presents a "Vedāntic Key" to the Gospels. This was by far the best interpretation of the Gospels by a Hindu *guru* that I have ever read.

More than anything else, the book *Christ The Guru* has helped me a great deal in integrating the spiritual wisdom of the Advaita Vedānta with the Gospel of liberating love of Lord Jesus Christ whom I have accepted as the "Sadguru" in my pilgrimage of faith and spiritual quest in the multireligious context of India. Hence, I was very happy to see that Swami Muni Narayana Prasad has also identified Lord Jesus Christ as "Sadguru" in his remarkable book.

This article is written as a loving tribute to Swami Muni Narayana Prasad for the "Guru Muni Śatābhiṣeka Smaraṇika". "Sadguru Christology", which is the central theme of this article, is the basic constituent of the "Indian face of the Christian faith" developed and authored by me. It is in harmony with the Vedāntic vision presented by Swamiji in his book *Christ The Guru*. This article also includes an introduction to the "Indian face of the Christian faith" and a liberative spirituality termed *sahana-yoga* demonstrated and taught to the world by Sadguru Jesus Christ along with a socio-spiritual ideology termed *tyāgārcana* derived from the liberative spirituality of *sahana-yoga*. The article concludes with a call addressed to the disciples of Sadguru Jesus Christ, Narayana Guru and Mahatma Gandhi in Kerala to join hands in the mission of an Integral Renaissance of India beginning with and from Kerala based on the liberative spirituality of *sahana-yoga* and the socio-spiritual ideology of *tyāgārcana*.

An Indian Face of the Christian Faith

By the term "Christian faith" I mean an abiding faith in the one true God revealed to humanity by Lord Jesus Christ, the Divine Master, through his own life and in his own being. It is also the faith that accepts and acknowledges Lord Jesus Christ as the "Word of God" incarnated on earth (John 1:14). Christian faith further implies accepting and acknowledging the Divine Master as the "human face of God" in history (John 14:9) and as "the way, the truth and the life" in humanity's eternal quest for God and His Kingdom on earth (John 14:6; Matt. 6:10). "Kingdom of God" was the vision and mission of Sadguru Jesus Christ. This term appears more than 100 times in the Gospels.

The Christian faith has acquired a number of "faces" in its evolutionary growth over the last two millennia. The first was a "Jewish face" which had presented Jesus of Nazareth as the "Lamb of God who takes away the sins of the world". This Jewish "face" was given to Jesus of Nazareth based on the Old Testament narratives of the "fall and redemption" of humankind and the concept of "original sin".

Next to the "Jewish face" came the "Roman face" which had presented Jesus of Nazareth as a "King" and "Saviour". The Jews were under the Roman rule at that time and they were eagerly waiting for a powerful king to liberate them from the Roman subjugation. Many of his disciples and followers had expected Jesus of Nazareth to be such a king and saviour.

However, it was the "Greek face" that had enabled the Christian faith to open up to the non-Jewish world by presenting Jesus of Nazareth as the "Christos" and "Logos". The Greek word *Christos* implies the "anointed one of God". The English word "Christ" has its origin in this Greek word. The Greek word *Logos* implies the "Word of God". In Indian terms it implies the Primordial Word, *Śabda-Brahman* or *ādi śabda*.

After a few centuries emerged the exclusive "Colonial face" of the Christian faith that proclaimed Christianity as the "only true religion" and the Bible as the "only true Word of God". Such exclusive claims which have no Biblical foundations and which are opposed to reason, led to conflicts and violence. Saving the souls of "pagans" by converting them to this colonial version of Christianity became the self-proclaimed obsession of European Christian missionaries and their counterparts and followers all over the world. This exclusive "Colonial face" which satisfies the religious ego of its proponents is the most widely spread face of the Christian faith in the world today. This is because the European colonial powers had conquered and ruled over a large number of countries in the world. Christian missionaries with the help and support of these colonial powers succeeded in spreading this "Colonial face" of the Christian faith all over the world.

The latest face of the Christian faith is the "Commercial face". It has its roots in the American competitive consumerist culture. This "Commercial face" proclaims Jesus of Nazareth as the Lord of wealth and wellness, and as the giver of all good things in life. It makes preaching the "Gospel of Wellness & Prosperity" a highly profitable and competitive business with a great deal of sound and fury. Consumerist societies like Kerala and Goa have been very fertile grounds for this version of the Christian faith.

The Christian faith that is being promoted in India and all over the world today by various Christian churches is based on one or more of the above five "faces" acquired by it over the centuries of its evolutionary growth. Unfortunately, none of the above five faces of the Christian faith appeals to the educated and religious-minded Indians (most of whom are Hindus) because these are not in harmony with India's religious genius that has ever been seeking for God and Truth incessantly with sincerity, simplicity and humility from time immemorial.

Christianity in India urgently needs an "Indian face" without religious conversion and cultural alienation and which is in harmony with India's own rich religious and spiritual traditions and insights as pointed out by E. Stanley Jones in his book *Christ of the Indian Road*. Such an "Indianized" Christianity must be rooted deep in the spiritual insights of the four

Gospels, and in an Advaitic vision of life and reality. (*NB*: Please refer to chapter 7 of my book *A New Creation in Christ* for details of the "Indian Face of the Christian Faith" and its constituents developed by me.)

Sadguru Christology

"Sadguru Christology" is the basic constituent of the "Indian face of the Christian faith" developed and authored by me. The term "Christology" implies the theological interpretation of the person and mission of Lord Jesus Christ. The term *sadguru* in the context of our mission implies true *guru* who is one with God and who is the power and wisdom of God ever active in history to lead humanity from falsehood to truth, from darkness to light and from death to eternal life. The qualities and characteristics of the *sadguru* are outlined in the following verses from Viśvasāra Tantra:

> *brahminānandam parama sukhadam kevalam jñāna* ।
> *mūrtim dvandvātītam gagana sadṛśam tattvamasyādi* ।।
> *lakṣyam ekam nityam vimalam acalam sarvadhīsākṣī bhūtam* ।
> *bhāvātītam triguṇarahitam sadgurum tam namāmi* ।।

> I bow to the True Guru who is the embodiment of the Bliss of God; Who bestows supreme happiness; the Absolute Who is Wisdom Incarnate; Who is beyond any duality; Who is vast like the sky; Whom "Thou Art That" and similar Scriptural verses have in view; Who is the One, the Eternal, the Pure, the Immovable, the Witness to all; Who is beyond all *bhāva*s, and devoid of the three *guṇa*s.

A critical and prayerful reflection on the qualities and characteristics of *sadguru* presented in the above verses will show to us clearly that the *sadguru* is none other than an "Incarnation" of God in human history. Hence, the *sadguru* Christology is an "Advaitic" Christology. The term *sadguru* is also the best suited title and identity for Lord Jesus Christ from an Indian socio-religious perspective. Muni Narayana Prasad also has identified Lord Jesus Christ as *sadguru*. The "Indian face of the Christian faith" has this "Sadguru Christology" as its "corner stone".

Liberative Spirituality of Sadguru Jesus Christ

"Spirituality" implies here the process of living one's life in communion with the one true God, the omnipotent, omnipresent and omniscient Supreme Spirit. Sadguru Jesus Christ taught that "God is Spirit" (John 4:24). "Spirituality" also implies a living and loving communion with God as one's own eternally loving and ever-forgiving Heavenly Parent (Matt. 6:8-15, Matt. 7:9-11; Luke 10:21-22).

Selfishness, pride, greed, lust and anger are the five major forces of evil (*duṣṭa śakti pañcakam*) blocking humanity's spiritual progress towards its final destiny which is to be one with God, the source of all life and ground of all existence. These forces of evil are very active both in the individual and collective dimensions of human life. These are also present and active in our religious, political, economic and social systems and institutions. Liberating oneself and others from these forces of evil is essential for our spiritual progress towards our ultimate destiny in the divine plan. The path of liberation from evil forces and structures and systems demonstrated and taught to the world by Sadguru Jesus Christ is the path of forgiving, enduring and self-sacrificing love which we have termed as *sahana-yoga*. It is the path of the "Cross".

Sahana-yoga mukti-mārga (the path of forgiving, enduring and self-sacrificing love is the path of liberation) is the eternal spiritual law demonstrated and taught to the world by Sadguru Jesus Christ. Mahatma

Gandhi understood this divine law of Christ very well and applied it effectively as *satyāgraha* for the political freedom of India. Until Gandhiji's time, the Western Christian world had thought, taught and accepted the teachings of Sadguru Jesus Christ as mere pious platitudes. But Mahatma Gandhi demonstrated to the world the power and wisdom of God in the "Cross of Christ". It is an irony of history that it took an unassuming Hindu "half-naked *fakīr*" to teach the mighty and arrogant Western Christian world the power and wisdom of God in the Cross of Christ! (Please refer to chapter III of my book *Bharatiya Dharma Rajya: Vision of Kingdom of God in India* and chapter 7 of *A New Creation in Christ* for details of *sahana-yoga*). We have developed a creative and liberative application of the eternal spiritual law of Christ in the context of the present pandemic-devastated world as an interreligious *sādhana* and socio-spiritual ideology of liberation termed *tyāgārcana*. The terms *tyāgārcana* is comprised of two words, *tyāga* and *arcana*. *Tyāga* means renunciation or sacrifice. It is used here to mean voluntary renunciation of something that is dear to one's heart. *Arcana* means an offering made to God with love. Selfless service rendered to our needy fellow human beings with love is the best form of *arcana* that we can offer to God. We can see God only in and through others. Hence, serving others with love is serving God with love. "Just as you did it to one of the least of these, you did it to me", affirmed Sadguru Jesus Christ (Matt. 25:40). *Mānava sevā, mādhava sevā* (service to humanity is service to God) is an ancient Indian dictum that reflects this teaching of Sadguru Jesus Christ. (Please refer to chapter V of *Bharatiya Dharma Rajya*: *Vision of Kingdom of God in India* and to chapter 4b of *Integral Renaissance of India* for details of *tyāgārcana*.)

Conclusion

India has a divine mission to fulfil in the world. It is to guide humanity in the path of *satya, dharma* and *śānti* (truth, righteousness and peace) based on an Advaitic vision of life and reality, and on an all-inclusive Earth Family Consciousness (*vasudhaiva kuṭumbakam*). The "Indian face of the Christian faith" with its *sadguru* Advaitic Christology and the *sahana yoga* liberative spirituality and *tyāgārcana* socio-spiritual ideology outlined above in this article can provide the much-needed "soul-force" and spiritual dynamism for awakening and empowering India to her destined divine mission in the world. An interreligious movement for Integral Renaissance of India under the name "Navasrushti India Mission" is being promoted by us for this purpose through a Moral Regeneration Force termed "Dharma Rajya Vedi" (DRV). My latest book *Integral Renaissance of India* serves as a mission manual for DRV and Navasrushti India Mission. Kerala is chosen as a pilot project by DRV in this historic divine mission. The Navasrushti Kerala Mission was initiated by DRV on 30 January 2021 from Dharma Bharathi Ashram as the Kerala pilot project of the Integral Renaissance of India/Navasrushti India Mission. The goal of Navasrushti Kerala Mission is to transform Kerala into a "Caitanya Keralam", a God's own country' of "one caste, one religion and one God for humankind" as envisioned by Narayana Guru. The liberative spirituality of *sahana yoga* and the socio-spiritual ideology of *tyāgārcana* ideology will provide the "soul force" for this divine mission. The disciples of Sadguru Jesus Christ, Narayana Guru and Mahatma Gandhi in Kerala are called to join hands and work together with DRV for realizing this goal of the Navasrushti Kerala Mission so as to make Kerala a God's own country in the true sense of the term. The verdict of history will be passed and the destiny of humanity will depend on the courage that the disciples of Sadguru Jesus Christ, Narayana Guru and Mahatma Gandhi in Kerala display in the coming years to make this mission of the era (Yuga Dharma) bear abundant fruits for the glory of God and good of humanity.

18

Caitanya Jyotis (Dynamic Effulgence)

Swami Tyageswaran

Now You are here as an experiencing universe
to see with eyes and to hear with ears.

Many are Your ways of knowing through smell, taste, etc.
Filling up I and the other is You, your Self.

Looking to see You, You are hiding in the eye.
Desiring to know You, again, You are hiding in the knowledge itself.
This is a wonder.

As You are in a state of fullness, filling all as a single entity;
there is no room to move. Hence, You are stillness.
In order to appear as each and everything in the world, as it is,
You unmovingly become the Mover.

How numerous are the modes of You that assume different ways
for understanding the forms of the world,
like day and night, as Your time form.
Is it necessary to mention morning and dusk, even night,

and the seasons like spring and autumn?
In such a way You have become a world-festival of zeal.

You have become the world and myself with all peculiar forms,
and omniscient.
Starting with me and ending with You.

Your Being is full and I reside in it.
Your state of "I-ness" is even more wonderful.
Breathing and blood circulation are your subtle actions.

How many more are the subtle processes
in the inner body to keep life going?
These numerous peculiar actions in the subtle body
include the nine aesthetic sentiments of life.
Happiness and sorrow.

You are not inside or outside; both and both not.
You are everywhere.

Here and in me, there and in them;
always everywhere
as dynamic effulgence (Chaitanya Jyotis).

Thou art manifested in the stillness of silence
The universe that sounds like the movement of the world,
The motion dissolved in meditation,
The sound manifested in awakening
The cosmic form
The secret place where creation is possible
You gently open into a dream.

19

Mahā Guru

Swami Tyageswaran

You are the rising sun in the sky above,
a blooming lotus in the lake below.
This ever-increasing brilliance of Yours is this universe,
that has become the celebration in the hearts of all humanity.

From the unseen, You become the power of imagination
to reveal yourself as the universe.
You are the Mother Earth for all beings
You are space for the sun and the moon.

Before the beginning when You were too subtle to be perceived
You become the Self-Created One, appearing as the world
and the universe
You took the form of Rishi *Poet like Vālmīki and Vyāsa.*
Later the compassionate Buddha
Again you changed the region and time of your birth and
became Jesus Christ and Prophet-Nebi,
now You Narayana Guru.

You reveal the world for mortals and
the Refuge for its refugees longing for immortality.
You are the embodiment of the union of jñāna *and* yoga,
The sparkling rays of Self-Sun.
The rare nature of your birth, samādhi *and* śānti,
are only modulations in the body.
You are the wisdom light
for entire humanity.

As the sayings indicate, this man that man, are of the same
content as this world.
By knowing this, You become the very mode of Self-happiness.
Whatever you want to do for yourself; should be good for others, also.
Such a direction you give.

Of one kind, one religion and one God for man;
this great saying is applicable to the entire humanity.
Even though we see differences in all beings –all beings have
only one Ātman,
on Self-realizing which, we know we are only one entity.

You gave a divine life star, the Brahma-mantra,
He who loves is who really lives
"Do repeat this sacred syllables nine by heart in place of lettered-charm."

You introduced many great Selves, the compassionate ones,
as shining examples for history.

You, by dispelling the ignorance of darkness and shedding the
grace of the white, cool sheen of light's elixir,
remove the ocean of limitless sorrows and help us regain

the immortal ocean of bliss, and merge into it.
In such a way, you become Mahā Guru.

We salute you again and again for the sheen of the full moon
that we can taste and feel.

Even though you are the embodiment of Self-happiness,
please shed your grace so that this will be revealed to us.

കേരള സാഹിത്യ അക്കാദമി
2017 ജൂൺ 10, 11
60-ാം

20

Rain Inside

Rani Jayachandran

Deep in my heart
It started to rain.
A heavy downpour
Of enigmatic sorrows
And the trials of life.
Mere wilderness!

Sleep will not claim me,
I'm sure.
I'm unsure of everything
Including the moonrise.
In this pathless night
I long to see you
At least for once.

Emotions run
Sober and deeper
But time started
Galloping faster.

In this blueness
Before sunrise
I hear your knock
Your call
I feel you approach
With the words
Of everlasting peace.

Now …
I'm not baffled
My emotions
I can contain.
The dreams
Of my quietest moments
I figure out
To go beyond this bay.

While gazing out
Through the wavy pane of life

Again I see saffron
At the edge of the sky.

The overlashed eyes
Of an empathetic sun
Started glancing at me.
An invigorating glance!
Transcends
All enslavements!

The silvery glaciers
Of my heart awaken
And melt
Into a million streams.

Emanates a new energy
And rhythm
In every breath
Of my being.
It illumines my heart
Elevates my thought.
It makes me understand
Who I am.

Now I hear
Only an exhilarating music.
The music from ...
Every blade of grass
Blooming flowers
Awakening buds
And glacial streams.
The symphony of God!
The symphony of Nature!

I wander off again
To talk to trees and birds
Grass and grapevine.
Deep in my heart
It started to rain.
A rain of mellow marigolds!
A rain of mellow yellow marigolds!

21

A Silent Seeker

Rani Jayachandran

It's twilight
The day weds the night.
The mighty painter
Pours out millions of colours
Silver, golden, crimson red …

The serenity of sandhyā bhāṣā
Its grammar
Of transformation
And generation
Its diminishing notes
Ascending …
Descending…

A … u … ṁ …
The moments
Of divine ecstasy!
Truth, Eternity and Beauty
The inseparable aspects of Almighty

In and around!

Energy flows equally
In my right and left.
All egos unveil
And sublimate.
Vanishes the whirlpool of miseries
And heart becomes
A multicoloured spectrum
That emanates
The abiding bliss within.

The subtler levels of beauty
Penetrates deep in my soul.
Words fail to roll down
From my lips.

Only my heart speaks:
"This is the Land of the Lord"!
I'm in a trance!
And I sink
Spontaneously into silence!